FROM THE GOSPEL OF ST. MATTHEW 8:7-8

"I will come myself and heal him," Jesus said. The Centurion replied, "Sir, I am not worthy to have you under my roof; say but the word and my servant will be healed."

FROM THE ROMAN MISSAL, "THE RECEPTION OF COMMUNION"

The Celebrant proclaims:
This is the Lamb of God
Who takes away the sins of the world.
Happy are those who are called to His Supper.

The Celebrant and people pray together:
Lord, I am not worthy to receive you,
but only say the word and I shall be healed.

also by Theodore E. Dobson
published by Paulist Press

INNER HEALING: GOD'S GREAT ASSURANCE
HOW TO PRAY FOR SPIRITUAL GROWTH

Theodore E. Dobson

SAY BUT THE WORD

How the Lord's Supper Can Transform Your Life

PAULIST PRESS
New York/Ramsey

Library of Congress
Catalog Card Number: 84-80355

ISBN: 0-8091-2635-4 (paper)
     0-8091-0355-9 (cloth)

Published by Paulist Press
545 Island Road, Ramsey, N.J. 07446

Printed and bound in the
United States of America

CONTENTS

FOREWORD *by Morton Kelsey* vii

1. EUCHARIST WITH OPEN HANDS 1

2. A SACRIFICE OF PRAISE 10

3. RECEIVING THE WORD 20

4. A SACRIFICE OF SELF 30

5. A UNION OF HEARTS 45

6. EUCHARIST CAN BE LIFE-CHANGING . . . 54

7. EUCHARIST: THE FIRST HEALING
   SERVICE OF THE CHURCH 66

8. TRANSFORMING THE WORLD
   THROUGH EUCHARIST 81

9. THE POWER OF EUCHARISTIC LOVE 93

10. RESOLVING DIFFICULTIES WITH
    EUCHARISTIC CELEBRATION 100

    appendix A
    AN OUTLINE FOR EUCHARISTIC
    CELEBRATION 116

    appendix B
    NOTES FOR CELEBRANTS 121

v

To Kathy, Phil, Ray and Mary
who walk the spiritual journey with me
and keep me honest

FOREWORD

Eucharist is the central Christian act of worship. Jesus himself instituted this service the night he was betrayed. The common meals which the disciples shared with their master had a mysterious significance which was revealed at that Passover meal. In addition the resurrected Jesus twice met his friends and disciples in the breaking of the bread. The early Christians met together regularly to share bread and wine and to give thanks (for Eucharist means to give thanks) for Jesus' sacrifice on Golgotha and for the fear-shattering victory of the resurrection. They found that the risen Christ was present with them at these celebrations in a unique way. These common times together to pray and worship and receive the sacrament were so important to those first Christians that they risked their lives to come to them. Most of those thrown to the lions in the arena were seized worshiping at their services of Eucharist.

In this book Father Dobson gives significant answers to two very important questions: Why doesn't this service have the same compelling attraction to modern Christians? How can we regain the depth and transforming power of Eucharistic celebration? He addresses both priests, with suggestions for celebrating this service, and the laity, giving practical methods by which they can enter more deeply into its mystery.

The author first of all turns our attention to Carl Jung's profound psychological analysis of Eucharist found in "Transformation Symbolism in the Mass" in Volume 11 of his collected works. Jung states that the Christian service of Holy Communion is one of the finest examples of the process of sacrifice and transformation that is at the heart of psychological and spiritual growth. At the very core of the human psyche Jung found the need for transformation, and he had discovered no human ritual meeting this need more adequately than the Eucharist.

Father Dobson points out that many Christians have forgotten the power of symbols and images in their praying. They are caught up in a secular, materialistic world and they come to Communion unconsciously either out of habit or because they want to get something for themselves. They do not realize that the Eucharist is essentially a service of self-giving and transformation enabling them to come to their divine potential and then to go out into the world sharing the good news, the love and healing power that the crucified and risen Jesus came to give. When, like the early Christians, our lives are at stake each time we come to Eucharist, we do not need to be reminded of sacrifice. Empowered Christianity has nearly always flourished in times of persecution.

The central message of *Say But The Word* is that we can bring ourselves, our souls and bodies as a living sacrifice to God *consciously* as we come to Holy Communion. We can then be empowered and transformed; we don't have to wait for persecution for this service to be filled with mystery.

Jung has written that the Catholic dogmatic system is the finest therapeutic system that has been given to human beings, and that it provides for every human psychological need. The finest expression of the wholeness of orthodox Christian faith is to be found in progression of the Eucharistic action. In addition the Mass meets our deepest spiritual needs. I would agree with Jung that the highest levels of psychological maturity and spiritual wholeness have much in common; we cannot separate them without danger to our souls. Personally I have found that the Eucharist has become more and more central to my life as I have come to understand more of the Christian Gospel. This service has become the daily focus of my praying and doing.

Father Dobson takes us step by step through the Eucharist. We begin with praise for the ability to come before God. Then as we come before the Holy One we will inevitably reflect upon our failures, ugliness and deliberate evil. We are people with unclean lips. Only Christianity offers free forgiveness for the sincere and heartfelt asking, and absolution is given to us. The Word of God is then present to us as we listen to the words of the Bible; the Word is alive and can speak to whatever specific need or concern we bring to the Eucharist. After this preparation we are given a time in which we offer intercessions and petitions. The sacrifice then follows, the sacrifice of our gifts of bread and wine and of ourselves as well. The author points out that sacrifice means giving without expecting anything in return. At this point, as we make our sacrifice of ourselves in our way as Christ offered himself in his way, transformation can take place.

With transformation there is often healing of mind, body and soul. Healing is part of the Eucharist. The body and blood of Christ are the medicine of immortality. Father Dobson shows clearly the essential nature of exchanging our greetings of peace with one another before we receive the elements of Communion. In order to receive the risen Lord fully in the sacrament we must be willing to sacrifice our lack of forgiveness. Jesus has told us that we are his followers when we love one another as he has loved us.

This book is written simply and clearly. All those who wish to look more deeply into the mystery of Eucharist will be able to understand it, and they will find general and specific suggestions on how to make this mystery more a part of their lives.

Morton Kelsey
Lent 1984,
Gualala, California

one

EUCHARIST WITH OPEN HANDS

Celebrating Eucharist with open hands is an attitude of faith. It is becoming conscious of who we are and sacrificing ourselves to God in the Eucharistic rite, in union with and imitation of Jesus' selfless sacrifice, expecting nothing in return except to be one with God. This communion with our Father produces a profound transformation of self that both heals and renews us, giving us more life than we could ever ask for or imagine.

I experienced most poignantly what it means to celebrate Eucharist with open hands a few years ago while attending a Christian conference of professionals. It was a critical moment in my life, because I had been giving so much of myself to people in many different circumstances, but the people with whom I was living were unable to give me the affirmation I needed, and I was unable to receive from them what they were able to give. I felt isolated and lonely, and in my loneliness I turned inward so that I came to the point of demanding that people give to me what I had given to others.

In this selfish attitude I sought out people at the conference only to have them listen to me talk of my frustration. Most of them were kind enough to do so, but after I finished each conversation, I only felt worse. As good as these people were, nothing they could do for me filled that inner emptiness, for it had been created by my attitude toward months and months of alienation. I felt hopeless—it was an inner sinking feeling that twisted my stomach, and that separated me from everyone around.

On the first evening of the conference we celebrated Eucharist, the Sacrament of the Lord's Supper. The celebrant of that Eucharist had recognized that many people at the conference were hurting from the pressures of their professional work and personal lives, and he was trying to help all of us bring this pain to the Lord in a creative and redemptive way. He suggested we identify with Jesus in Gethsemani, for there He found the strength to endure pain while still retaining His integrity and wholeness, and throughout the ordeal that was to follow He never lost faith in His Father, even though He did seem to feel He had lost contact with Him.

His suggestion helped me offer my experience of loneliness and selfishness to the Father as my gift at that Eucharist, precisely in the way we are going to discover in this book. I identified my inner pain with the gifts of bread and wine; and when the bread and wine became the Body and Blood of Jesus, I believed that my pain entered His heart, where all healing and renewal begin. As I received Communion, I asked Jesus what He was doing to fill my inner emptiness and renew my connection with people. I sensed that His response was twofold: opening my heart to give others the same love I was seeking from them, just as He had done on the way to the Cross, and also asking that for the rest of the conference I put myself aside as much as possible. This I began to do immediately as well as I could.

By the next morning I already began to feel the effect of Eucharist the night before. In loving and affirming others, I was giving them the freedom to love and affirm me as they were able, without manipulating it. In trying to understand their lives, my own need for understanding was receding.

But during a break between sessions, a clearer effect of the sacrifice I had made in union with Jesus was revealed. The person who was responsible for the conference Eucharists asked me to celebrate that night. His request offered me a way to give a gift to everyone there. When I had come to the conference, I had wanted to be the center of attention; by sacrificing that desire in Eucharist, I found instead the wholeness I needed to be other-centered. By giving my heart to others, I learned how to be the focus of people's attention without being selfish, and I found I was happier than I could ever have been by focusing on my own need.

From that conference I went home to the people who could not affirm me, and there I had a second opportunity to find out how powerful Eucharist could be to transform my life.

At that time I was living in a house with several priests, one of whom was an elderly man with a heart condition. He and I had had a difficult relationship for most of the time we had been living there. It began when we discovered we were usually on opposing sides of issues. Soon we found it difficult to talk with each other, then to relate with each other, and finally simply to be with each other. Just before I had left for the conference, he and I had had a particularly angry discussion, of which both of us were ashamed but about which neither of us yet had done anything to reconcile.

Soon after I came home I found myself in the pew during a Eucharist which this priest was celebrating. As I watched him, my old feelings of animosity toward him began to rise up unbridled. But when this occurred I decided to look at my feelings of hurt and anger in light of the Cross and the meaning of Eucharist. I was filled with shame for myself and my reactions to him. Struggling against pride which resisted admitting I had been wrong, I offered our relationship to the Lord in the way we are about to investigate in this book. Through prayer and intentionality I identified with the bread the angry words that had marked our relationship and with the wine the feelings of hurt and anger in my heart, asking forgiveness for all. When the bread and wine became the Body and Blood of Jesus I believed that our relationship, including all of the difficulties in it, were in His heart and that He would begin to heal it through grace. By Communion I was begging God for a reconciliation and asking Him what I could do to accomplish it.

The next time I saw that priest, he was having a difficult time walking up some stairs because of his poor heart. I offered to walk with him and he let me do it. From that point on we were able to talk with each other again. Through the self-sacrifice that is Eucharist, the Sacrament of the Lord's Supper, God had worked the miracle of forgiveness in both of us.

Whether we call this ceremony Holy Communion, the Lord's Supper, Mass, or Eucharist (from the Greek prefix *eu* which means "good" and the word *charis* which means "beautiful" or "gift," and which, when put together, came to mean "thanksgiving" or "to give thanks"), it is really much more than a ceremony; it is a celebration that can transform our lives.

There are many people who celebrate Eucharist weekly, even daily in some traditions, but who do not see or receive the power that is there. Some merely "attend" and do not participate; others see it as "the time they give to God" and choose to relate with Him only through this sense of obligation to give Him something; others treat the Eucharist as a ceremony to be performed well so that it yields an aesthetic experience; still others see it as a social gathering drawing people together in community.

But in the earliest Christian days, the Eucharist was seen as a Sacrament of healing and transformation, a rite that brought wholeness to the people who celebrated it. For example, St. Augustine in his greatest book, *The City of God*, as well as in his last book, *Revisions*, witnessed to the healing he had seen in his own church as a result of people receiving Eucharist. He did not think it strange that true worship of God should yield positive, palpable results in the bodies, minds, spirits, and relationships of those who were participating in it, and, through their love and intercession, in the lives of others for whom participants would pray. Truly, in those days Eucharist was seen by many as the healing service of the Church.

Yet today that knowledge seems to be lost, and so people go without the help they need in their daily lives—help that is readily available to them in this form of worship of God. Through this book we will attempt to reconnect with these Christian roots, but by using approaches that are distinctive to the twentieth century. As we investigate the transforming and healing power of the Lord's Supper, we will see how celebration of Eucharist can affect our lives positively:

- Eucharist can bring us to consciousness, resulting in personal psychological wholeness;

- Eucharist calls us to imitate Christ's self-sacrificing love, leading us into holiness;

- Eucharist can bring us into physical wholeness, sometimes immediately, but more often over a period of time receiving the Sacrament in faith;

- Eucharist can bring us new hope for the transformation and healing of broken relationships;

- Eucharist can be a way to pray effectively for the transformation of our world, or, in other words, a way to intercede for loved ones, to bring healing for people's illnesses, and to improve their situations as they suffer from the effects of evil.

In this book, then, we will investigate the various elements of Eucharistic celebration, seeing how they combine to offer us the renewal and transformation we seek not only for ourselves but also for the world. In other words, we will examine that which is familiar to us—maybe too familiar—as we look at each part of the celebration to find out how it contributes to the "healing service" that Eucharist is, not only on a personal level but also on a corporate level, that is, as the Body of Christ.

We will also examine how the Lord's Supper can address the different needs in our lives, applying our understanding of the renewing nature of this worship to specific situations, and seeing how these prayers, when they are prayed sincerely, can bring us into the life (grace) we seek. We will see that Eucharist is meant to bring us to greater consciousness of ourselves as well as of how we are responding to the world and to the life God is giving us. We will also see that it is meant to bring us to a greater consciousness of our spiritual power in Christ to affect both the world within and the world around us. But most of all, we will see that Eucharist leads us to true spirituality as it invites us to sacrifice ourselves to the Father as Jesus does.

These reflections on Eucharist come out of a long love affair I have had with the Sacrament. Ever since I was a child, Eucharist has been the way I have met God most frequently and most deeply. Since my ordination as a priest I have continued to find it the most meaningful spiritual experience in my life. I am in love with the Eucharist, for it is the continuing experience of God living among us. It is a way we can mystically enter into Jesus' death and resurrection, so that we can accept His saving grace into our hearts in the lifelong process we call salvation. I continue to find that Eucharist is a mystery to be uncovered and revealed, not an object to be examined. I find, too, that my love for God grows most every time I celebrate it; and each Eucharist under different circumstances, with different people, for different needs and purposes, reveals a new dimension of this living celebration.

This book is written, therefore, to help all of us love the Eucharist more. In one special way it is for people who already love the Eucharist, but who want their experience of God in this celebration to be as vital and alive as possible. In another way, it is written for people who do not see any vitality or life in the celebration at all, who attend Eucharist for obligatory or social purposes, or who have ceased participating in Eucharist because they see no value or worth to the rite. To help them investigate the gift and the work that Eucharist is may enkindle in them a love for this ceremony as well. This book is also written for people involved in preparing or celebrating Eucharist, not only to help them in their ministry to others, but also to assist them in their ever-growing need to love the ceremony that is their ministry.

For the original kernel of insight into the transforming and healing power of the Eucharist which first inspired the contents of this book, I am indebted, not to a theologian or a spiritual leader, but to the Swiss psychologist Carl Jung who, in his monograph, "Transformation Symbolism in the Mass" (*Psychology and Religion: West and East*, Volume 11 of the Collected Works of C.G. Jung, Bollingen Series XX, Princeton University Press, pp. 201-298), takes a fresh look at the ceremony of the Lord's Supper from a psychological point of view. While much of his material is not relevant to our topic here, certain passages are of great importance to an understanding of the dynamic by which Eucharist can bring us to wholeness and holiness.

In this work, Jung never claims to be commenting on the spiritual issues involved in Eucharist, only on the human or psychological. But on that level—a level on which he is among the most competent to speak—he pays the Eucharistic rite, as well as the Roman Catholic Church which has preserved and developed it, his highest compliment. Jung called the process of maturing and integration of the personality "the process of individuation," and said it was the great work of every human being's life. In this treatise he describes the Eucharist as "the rite of the individuation process" (p. 273), explaining what he means in detail. With these words he states his belief that Eucharist is the supreme corporate religious activity through which people can become whole and complete human beings.

Jung's treatise, therefore, gives psychological credibility to the rite of the Eucharist because it unfolds the valid psychological truths which underlie it. It demonstrates the fact that this celebration gives spiritual expression to basic psychological needs in human beings.

In studying this material I have sorted out those parts that relate to the spiritual life, and these principles have been applied to the rite as it exists today (Jung wrote this work in 1954 before the liturgical reform of the Second Vatican Council). The result is an approach to Eucharistic celebration that has made it come alive for many to whom it has been presented as a lecture or a retreat conference. These people have found that this approach opens them to new dimensions of a familiar ceremony. And after one or two years many continue to say that they have been applying this teaching in their worship regularly since they heard it with ever-increasing results: many different kinds of healing and personal transformation happen, bringing wholeness and holiness into their lives.

Wholeness and holiness will often be mentioned together in this book, but we need to note that they are not the same reality. Wholeness is something we work to achieve and it happens basically on the psychological level; holiness is a gift from God and is basically a spiritual relationship with Him whereby we identify with Him and imitate Him. It is sensible for us to say, however, that wholeness of our personalities gives us greater freedom to choose holiness. By wholeness we mean knowing the parts of ourselves well, so that the power of each is released and integrated into the complete self. In other words, wholeness means that we do not repress the functions of our personalities, and that we accept ourselves and live full lives.

Holiness, as a gift from God, is a work of grace and of

God's favor. It is relating with God so that we become like Him—selfless, caring, loving, spiritually strong. It is easier for us to develop this Christ-like identity if we are in touch with all the functions of our personalities so that they are able to assist us in the spiritual journey toward holiness.

Through this book we will come to understand how Eucharist can bring us to wholeness as well as to holiness. Since, as St. Thomas Aquinas said, grace builds on nature, we will look at the psychological dimensions of Eucharist so that we can more meaningfully experience its spiritual dimensions, through which we enter a most intimate union with Jesus Himself. We will approach Eucharist as a mystery to be uncovered rather than as an object to be examined. To appreciate both the psychological and spiritual nature of this search, therefore, we will need to proceed assisted by the twin strengths of understanding and faith.

two

A SACRIFICE OF PRAISE

The Eucharist is, at its roots, a Sacrament of transformation. While many people may never have seen the Eucharist this way, the rite itself is speaking the language of renewal and transformation throughout.

The most basic and obvious transformation that takes place in the Eucharist is the bread and wine becoming the Body and Blood of Christ. Without this transformation, it would be senseless to hope for any other. This is, as the Apostolic tradition phrases it, the "mystery of faith" (*mysterium fidei*), the wonder of God really present among human beings under the forms of bread and wine.

But other more personal transformations can take place as well, and to the degree to which we are conscious of what can happen in us through Eucharistic celebration, and to the degree to which we choose it to happen, Eucharist will begin to affect our lives. For example, on an individual level, God calls each of us through Eucharist to become more whole and holy—to become more the person He has always meant for us to be. This individual call to wholeness and holiness we will investigate more completely later, but basically it is the call to sacrifice ourselves to God with Jesus, and to undergo the same kind of transformation He has experienced. This is the structure and nature of the Eucharistic celebration.

On the corporate level, another transformation is possible. God assembles us as ordinary people and gives us the choice to become the Mystical Body of Christ on earth, the Church—that group of people who think, feel, and act in the power and personality of Jesus because He gives us His Spirit and His gifts. This indwelling of God empowers ordinary people to accomplish His divine will on earth because their unity in Him makes them strong enough to do it.

We can see, then, that the Lord's Supper is the ultimate rite of "humanization" (cf. Jung, pp. 262-65), that is, of becoming the best that a human being can be physically, psychologically, and spiritually. We need to be "humanized" because we are not entirely human, in the best sense of the word. It is strange that when we use the word "human" we often do so pejoratively, as in the statement, "I made a mistake, but after all, I'm only human." Truly, it is the weakness and darkness of our personalities that *keep* us from being fully human—attitudes of egocentricity, selfishness, pride, hostility toward other people, rebelliousness toward God's will, the desire to remain unconscious of our true selves, resistance toward personal growth, and not recognizing our own or others' giftedness. But these dimensions of our personalities can be humanized as we commemorate Jesus in the Eucharist.

For Eucharist is a commemoration of the Lord's Last Supper, and of His suffering, death, and resurrection. It is a way in which Jesus comes into our midst. For many people, commemorations are "deadening" experiences, merely asking the participants mentally to honor the memory of some praiseworthy person or group, or to honor some memorable event. We experience this type of "commemoration" when, for example, a famous person has died and we are asked to bow our heads in a minute of silence. Most of us do not know what to do at such a moment, because we are given no way truly to commemorate the person.

However, true commemorations draw the participants into that which is being commemorated—they are exciting and "enlivening" experiences because they energize our inner beings with the virtues and the beauty of the person(s) being celebrated, or with the wonder and importance of the event being remembered. An example of this type of commemoration would be a funeral of a great leader at which his own inspirational words are read. Another would be using pageants to retell the story of Jesus' birth at Christmas, or the history of our nation on the Fourth of July. In other words, these types of commemorations draw us into an inner experience which begins a process of transformation.

The commemoration that is the Lord's Supper is no different. Through the prayers and actions of the Eucharist, we are drawn into Jesus, we identify with Him, we honor and respect Him, we are energized by His love and holiness, and, most of all, we affirm our desire to become like Him, to be transformed. Eucharist humanizes us who are unwhole and incomplete, as we become one with Christ, the total human being. When Jesus said at the Last Supper, "Do this in memory of me" (Lk 22:19), this is indeed the kind of "remembering" to which He was referring. Through the celebration of Eucharist, we also remember (in this deepened sense) the great events that have given us new life in Christ.

These many kinds of transformation are a mystery that seize us—we do not "make them happen." They are a work of grace, of divine gift. They come to us because Eucharist is a sacrifice—Jesus' continuing sacrifice of Himself, and our own sacrifice of ourselves. For to sacrifice ourselves to God is the most Christ-like attitude we can attain, and it creates an intimate communion with Christ, the One Who heals and transforms.

To understand Eucharist, then, we need to know what we mean by "sacrifice." The meaning of this word is probably most clearly shown by the root words from which it comes: *sacrum facere*, which in Latin literally mean "to make sacred" or "to consecrate." We make something sacred, of course, by giving it to God Who is sacred. The Greek word for sacrifice, *thysia*, also adds a dimension to our understanding, for it has in it the notion of "burning" or of "flaring up"—this because of the leaping sacrificial fire by which the Greeks often offered gifts to their gods. This understanding of sacrifice was that the appearance of the gift had to be changed or destroyed.

To sacrifice, then, in its root form, means to make something sacred by giving it to God, in such a way that it changes, and at least feels as if it were being destroyed. We are given the opportunity to make this kind of sacrifice in the Eucharist with all the parts of our human selves—to make them sacred (and, therefore, whole and holy) by giving them to God so freely that we feel as if they were being destroyed. We will understand more clearly how such a self-sacrifice can bring transformation as we continue to explore the kind of sacrifice the Eucharist is, and to see the kind of sacrifice it demands from us.

In the first part of the Eucharistic celebration we sacrifice ourselves to God through praise in word and song. We sing to the Lord, confessing our faith in Him and our love for Him; and we pray various prayers aloud and silently which acknowledge Him as God, Creator, and Father of all.

Praise begins the transformation and healing process that is Eucharist. The dictionary defines praise as "an expression of approval, a commendation." To praise God simply means to think favorably of Him and to express it. Because we are body as well as mind and spirit, what is inside must sometime reach the outside if it is to become completely real. For example, our love for others would be no more than sentimental feelings if we never expressed it. To think that a child has done well on a project and not to tell her so leaves her unsure of herself and unaware of her success. She does not know that we love her and appreciate her until we say we do.

When it comes to praising God, He may know what is

going on in our inner selves, but we often do not know precisely what we think or the intensity of our feelings until we give expression to these inner realities. Therefore, only to praise Him inwardly denies us the benefits of praise. Furthermore, it is only through the expression of praise that we commit ourselves to it, that we "tell the world" what we think and feel about the person we are praising. Otherwise, if our praise is only silent, we are not allowing it to affect us or others' opinions of us. All of us are aware of how expressing our inner feelings commits us to them by the embarrassment we have when we have expressed an opinion that is not popular. I can remember, for example, the hours of self-doubt I could endure as a youngster after I had expressed a political point of view with strength and vehemence. I was sure that the people to whom I had spoken would not want to talk with me again because I had declared myself so strongly.

Many people say that to sing or pray aloud in church makes them feel ridiculous, and yet they may at other times find themselves cheering during a sports event for their favorite team or person, or expressing themselves in some other similar situation. Praising God aloud is expression of our love for Him, and love cannot grow unless it finds expression. For some of us, our problem with vocalized praise could be not a difficulty with expressing ourselves but rather an embarrassment with expressing *love*.

To praise God, then, means that we focus on Him with our entire selves—body, mind, and spirit. Doing this immediately draws us into a different world, the world of the wonder, beauty, and perfection of our God. Already, however, the decision to praise God is a sacrifice of ourselves, for to concentrate on Him necessitates that we forget about ourselves. We need to sacrifice our selfishness to enter into God's world of healing and transformation.

When we come together for worship, we are often caught

up in the concerns of our own lives—our problems, our pains and illnesses, our hurt feelings, and our guilt which, at its best, focuses us on our need to improve, and, at its worst, focuses us hopelessly on our own weakness. Immediately, God begins to change us through praise. He draws us out of ourselves and out of our selfish concern to enjoy the wonder of Him. He assembles us as the Body of Christ to praise Him. He draws us into community for praise because He knows it is easier to enter into joy and wonder with others. Each of us has experienced this truth in the frustration we have felt when others would not enjoy with us something that we appreciated. I can remember as an adolescent taking friend after friend to the Art Institute in Chicago hoping to find one who could see what I was seeing in my favorite paintings. Joy that is lonely loses the edge of the happiness it can otherwise bring.

In praise we are drawn out of ourselves to be present to God and to the people around us. Thus in praise we begin the work of self-sacrifice by giving to God concerns that keep our vision narrow and our faith weak. It hurts to think of something other than ourselves when we are in pain, even the slightest pain, and it is a sacrifice to do it. All we need do is remember how our last headache prevented us from being gentle and considerate to others to understand that truth.

But when we do move out of ourselves and focus our attention on another, our spirits begin to expand, in this case, trying to comprehend the glory of God. In this "expanded" state, we can begin to wonder whether, if not yet entirely to believe that, God through Eucharist could touch our pain with love strong enough to make us whole. Thus, we begin to be free of our concerns and ready for worship. We are allowing God to humanize us through our praise of Him. To experience this effect within us, however, our praise needs to be honest and sincere. We do not need to *feel* like praising God, or to feel wonderful because we are doing it, but we do need simply to focus our attention as much as we can on Him, and to express as well as we can our love for Him.

If praise means acknowledging God to be Who He is, then a second way of praising Him offered to us as we begin Eucharistic celebration is seeking His forgiveness for our sin. If we seek God's forgiveness we are acknowledging His right, His authority, and His desire to forgive us. Trusting His desire and ability to forgive us because He loves us compliments Him, expressing that approval, that commendation that is at the heart of praise.

Many people have difficulty seeking God's forgiveness simply because it involves becoming conscious of the way they live. By the word "conscious" we describe our awareness of ourselves—our personality characteristics, the past events of our lives, our talents, weaknesses, attitudes, feelings, thoughts, and behavioral tendencies—what can readily be called to mind. Similarly, by the word "unconscious" we describe all that we do not know or admit about ourselves; unconsciousness is by its nature mysterious and somewhat frightening to explore, for our search may reveal things about ourselves which, for many different reasons, we may not care to know.

These revelations may be of weaknesses that are embarrassing or confusing, attitudes that are selfish and narrow, feelings that are petty or violent, thoughts that are prejudicial or incomplete, or gifts and talents which may call us out of our comfortable way of living into a new world of creativity or service. Whatever else exploring our unconscious will do, it will suggest, even demand, change in our lives. For this reason there are people who decide that consciousness asks too much from them. For example, I remember an acquaintance who was having a difficult time relating to a relative of his, and he came to me with the problem. We talked about the possibility that his need was to forgive the other person. Later I came across a cassette tape on the topic of forgiveness which I thought might help him. After listening to it, he sharply informed me that I was the one who needed to forgive, never explaining what he meant by that statement, and he dropped the subject and never brought it up again.

People who act this way cannot seek God's forgiveness simply because they choose to be unconscious, to one degree or another, of the real reasons they themselves need to be forgiven. The pain of consciousness, of self-knowledge, seems to be more than they feel they can endure. Of course, this is true only if they are heavily invested in not changing. These people will come to God and admit little mistakes or "socially acceptable" faults, but admitting these does not cost them much. They can admit them and still keep their lives fairly much the way they want them. They are afraid God may ask of them something they do not want to do, so the best way they can remain secure is to keep their distance from God, not making themselves vulnerable to Him.

One convenient way people may acknowledge the need for confession without making themselves vulnerable to change is by asking forgiveness for "whatever in my life may be at fault." This kind of "generalized confession" (not *general confession*, which is a humble admitting of all the major areas of sinfulness in a person's life and personality) does nothing to bring people to consciousness regarding their darker selves, but it does relieve their consciences of the guilt that comes from not confessing at all. They can "feel good" about themselves because they have done what has been asked of them, but they have only obeyed the letter of the law and not fulfilled its spirit.

God asks us to seek forgiveness so that we can become conscious of what we are doing that is wrong and *change*, not so that we can play a game of confession while retaining our inviolable position of self-righteousness. (This principle also holds true in our human relationships—to ask someone's forgiveness for "whatever I may have done to hurt you" is not to ask forgiveness at all; unless there is some consciousness of what specifically we have done to hurt the other, are sorry for causing that pain, and are willing to change, we have not sincerely asked to be forgiven.)

True confession of the soul, a true seeking of God's forgiveness, is a sacrifice of the ego—that part of us that is our conscious sense of who we are as persons—and it is tantamount to admitting that we need to change, that we are not adequate. There is necessary pain in this act, but it is the pain of growth. The only alternatives to this pain are the immature security of psychic slumbering or the raging tumult of unresolved guilt.

The pain of saying that we are not entirely adequate—in other words, that we focus our lives on ourselves, and that our perspectives are narrow and therefore hurtful to others—is the pain that unites us with Jesus Who suffered and died and rose to be our adequacy. Our spiritual death is admitting our inadequacy. But if we will never be adequate on our own, and if we will always need God's forgiveness to heal us, His strength to overcome difficulties, and His transforming love to make us better individuals for ourselves and for the world in which we live, we need not feel hopeless, for God is always ready and willing to provide such help. Our spiritual resurrection is Jesus living within us. In Him we can be adequate.

So again we are humanized—we are made more complete as human beings—as we admit to God and to each other the truth of our lives. For the truth is twofold: Not only are we imperfect by ourselves, but also God makes us perfect through grace, that is, through His life in us. God's judgment is forgiveness.

God's forgiveness frees us to acknowledge the truth about ourselves. For many of us, seeking forgiveness creates fear because we insecurely feel that once we admit our sin before the Almighty and perfect God, He will destroy us, hurt us, or at least punish us. But He has solved the problem of our fear by forgiving us *before* we ever sinned. That His forgiveness is a "foregone conclusion" frees us not to be afraid of Him, but to be honest with Him. We know that His response to our honesty will not be punishment or pain (He knows that we have already felt pain in the act of being honest, and that our pain has brought us to Him in truth) but freedom and forgiveness.

Thus, God's forgiveness encourages us to be conscious of who we really are, and not to hide in unconsciousness our darker selves. Before Him we do not have to be afraid of our imperfection, and neither do we have to be afraid of our perfect God, although we can still choose to be afraid of both.

Praising God by seeking His forgiveness, then, continues to take our minds off our weakness and refocuses them on His love, drawing us into His world, seeing our lives from His more perfect perspective. We find that as we admit who we are before Him, we are transformed. Our inner selves are expanded in consciousness and holiness, the selfishness of our egos is diminished, and we are elevated to a new state of spirituality. When we have become more conscious of our real selves by seeking and receiving His forgiveness in the Eucharistic celebration, He is then able to lead us into the transformation, renewal, and healing that is to come in the continuation of this meeting with Him we call Eucharist.

three

RECEIVING THE WORD

In the Opening Rite of the Eucharistic celebration we praise God through word, song, and seeking His forgiveness. In this way we make ourselves vulnerable to God and all He is willing to do in us and through us. Our efforts to praise Him seek to make us as vulnerable as possible. Through them we are drawn more deeply into the transforming wonder of this ceremony of worship by the presence of Jesus, a presence which is intensified through our praise of Him.

The transformation that Eucharist promises has begun through our conscious decision to concentrate on God and be consumed less by ourselves. It now continues as we enter the first major part of the ceremony, the Liturgy of the Word, which consists of readings from the Bible, responses to those readings, and reflections on those readings, ordinarily called a homily or sermon. Praise has opened us to what God may have to say to us; now we listen to His Word and receive it into our hearts. His Word will continue the work of consciousness in us. It will heighten our awareness of who we are now as well as of who He is calling us to become. Again we see that receiving God's Word is a sacrifice of self on our part, for to hear it in our hearts is to be ready to change our inner and outer lives according to all that it says.

Sometimes when we read or hear the Bible we forget that it is not like any other book. Every other book is a series of words printed on pages that communicate the ideas, feelings, reactions and attitudes of the author who wrote it. But the Bible is different—it is more than that. The Sacred Scriptures are alive! "The word of God is alive and active..." (Heb 4:12). The Holy Spirit lives in the Bible making it vital and life-giving. This fact makes reading or hearing God's Word an extraordinary opportunity for healing, transformation, and renewal. If God Himself lives in that Word, then any time we come in touch with it we are connecting with God, the Source of all the good things we seek in our lives.

Another way that the Word of God is different from mere human words is that it has the power *to do what it says*! "The word that goes from my mouth does not return to me empty without carrying out my will and succeeding in what it was sent to do" (Is 55:11). Experiencing God's Word with openness and consciousness, then, makes it possible for it to be accomplished in our lives. This is one reason that in the New Testament Jesus frequently commends people for listening to His words (Mt 7:24-27), that He is frustrated with people who "listen without hearing" (Mt 13:13), and that He so frequently says, "Listen, anyone who has ears to hear!" (Lk 8:8).

For example, at a critical moment in my life I celebrated a Eucharist at which one of the readings was St. Paul's famous description of love in his First Letter to the Corinthians (13:1-13). The question I was facing then was whether I loved God enough to allow Him to give me a task I did not want to do. Hearing those words broke my defenses so completely that I not only gave Him permission to do whatever He wished with my life, but I also wanted to do what He wanted. My will and His were made one through the love for Him created in my heart by His own Word.

So God's Word is a creating word: "God said, 'Let there be light,' and there was light" (Gn 1:3). Similarly, God's Word has the power to create in us exactly what it describes—

righteousness, holiness, beauty, wonder, hope, faith, love, and all virtue and goodness.

We, however, have a difficult time believing that any word could be so powerful, simply because our notion of what a word is has been devalued by the way we ourselves use words. It used to be that a person's word was his or her bond, that people stood by their words. A friend of mine once told me how he learned this principle from his grandfather. In the farm country where he grew up, he witnessed his grandfather and other farmers trade hundreds of units of commodities merely by a word and a shake of the hand. Their trust in each man's integrity was the bond by which their community stayed together.

But it is far from so in most places today. We have learned to break promises and tell lies for expediency's sake. Many children think nothing from their earliest years of hiding the truth to protect themselves from being corrected. Furthermore, we are subject to advertising in which words are loosely used to sell rather than to tell the truth. From these kinds of experiences many have developed an unconscious attitude that words do not mean much, and that promises mean less. Therefore, when these people come to the Word of God, they are tempted to treat it no differently. Before they can believe it is true, they must test it and try it, and even then they are not sure it is worth all that trouble, because they expect to be disappointed by it.

However, the simple truth is that for God, His Word is His bond; for God, His Word does not come back to Him empty, but it always fulfills His intention.

If God through His Word will be able to create His image within us, however, we will need to receive that Word and submit to it. We will need to respond actively to what it says with gratitude and vulnerability. We will need to be the kind of people who "hear and listen," and not ones whose hearts have grown hardened to any influence but our own (cf. Mt 13:10-17). We cannot expect God to accomplish His Word in us if we are entirely closed. Yet if we sense that we are closed to God's

Word transforming our lives, we can recognize this fact and confess it honestly to the Lord in prayer, asking Him to find His way into our hearts and create His life within us through His love.

Because God's Word is alive and active, because God's Word is able to create what it says, and because God's Word is His bond, listening to and reflecting upon the Scriptures as they are read to us at this point in the Eucharistic celebration creates a unique opportunity for us. Receiving God's Word places us in a new relationship with God Himself. We are being vulnerable to His ability to heal and transform us. God's Word helps us to be conscious so that we can understand the decisions we must make to become whole and holy people, for it brings His truth to confront our falsehood, His guidance to confront our confusion, His hope to confront our apathy and despair, and His wisdom to help us resist conforming to empty values.

Falsehood, confusion, apathy, despair, and conforming to empty values are all human experiences, but they are not the best kind. We again find ourselves, therefore, at the point of needing to be humanized. God's Word is the humanizing agent, and our sacrifice of self—opening ourselves to change, with all the pain of self-knowledge that it involves—is our way of being vulnerable to God's work in us through His Word. As we thus acknowledge that we are truly among the poor in spirit, His Word can begin to change us. As we let ourselves and Him know the poverty of our own humanity, that is, that we are not all that we could be or all that He wants us to be, His Word can begin to address the needs for growth we have at this time.

Because God's Word is alive and active, filled with His life, the same reading from Scripture can speak to the hearts of different people with varying needs at the same time. For the Holy Spirit lives in that Word, and its purpose is to accomplish what it says. The same truth spoken at the same time can, under the guidance of the Spirit, enter each open heart precisely in the way that heart needs to hear it. The only predisposition necessary is to be *expecting* God's Word to make a difference when we hear it.

Expectation creates a human electricity that entirely transforms people and events. When Pope John Paul II visited the United States, I remember waiting on a warm fall day in an Iowa meadow with 350,000 other people for him to arrive by helicopter. Our expectation created an excitement that transformed many hours of waiting into a pleasant experience, and that opened us to the message he spoke and the prayer he prayed when he finally arrived.

Expecting to hear something that will have personal meaning for us is the simplest and most honest way we can open ourselves to the healing and transforming power of God's Word. Where there is no expectation there is no faith, and faith is the key to being made whole. "Everything is possible for anyone who has faith" (Mk 9:24). But our expectation is not of *what* God will say to us about our lives, but rather *that* He will say something of importance to us. Otherwise, we do not have expectation but rather a closedness to His sovereignty to speak that which He wishes. Having an expectation of *what* God will say keeps us from hearing anything new, and therefore keeps us confined to the limits of our own minds. But true expectation for God to speak to our hearts through His Word creates that anticipation by which His Word can make a difference in the way we live. That which has been unconscious and damaging in our lives comes to light. Also, through God's Word entirely new wisdom can come to us from the spiritual realm.

The Word of God, then, helps to make us more conscious of ourselves, our lives, and the meaning of our lives. Because God is Truth, His Word communicates the truth of ourselves to us, so that we can see more clearly what our conscious self-concept is and sacrifice it to God, receiving from Him a new and more expansive sense of ourselves.

God's Word is thus a mirror reflecting our inner selves back to us. In that mirror we can see both our selfishness as well as our growth. The Word of God transforms us and heals us of our egocentric attitudes and brings us into communion with others if we receive it sincerely.

For example, hearing God's Word can help us to see our errors and know how we can change. Remembering that God's Word does what it says, we realize that hearing this message will not impose on us impossibly high standards of behavior, but rather being open to God's Word will actually give us the ability to do what is right. The Word also can encourage us in our virtue and, similarly, give us the ability to grow in it. It can give us whatever we need at the time of hearing it to come to God with the fullest awareness possible of who we are and what our lives mean. With this consciousness we can give ourselves to Him as completely as possible.

We cannot give to God what we do not have. If we are not conscious of the exaltation of our virtue and the depth of our weakness and sin, we do not "have" a life to give to God freely and deliberately. We are not psychologically in possession of ourselves. So when the Word of God makes us more conscious, it is preparing us for the choice we must make at some time whether to live for God or to live for ourselves.

The Word of God is His wisdom, truth, and love for us, and when we open ourselves to the transforming power of this Word, admitting that we cannot live successfully guided by our own self-developed principles, we open our lives to being guided by these attributes. The more we receive His Word into our hearts without attempting to manipulate it to mean what we want it to mean or expect it to mean, the more we are formed in His wisdom, truth, and love. Also, the more His Word becomes a part of our lives the less power will confusion, doubt, fear, anxiety, hopelessness, and insecurity have in our lives. It is not that we can avoid these experiences, but they will not form our lives as they used to, to the degree to which we continue to receive His Word.

Of course, this openness is again a sacrifice of our selfishness and ego-centeredness, and that sacrifice allows us to grow as persons and as Christians. As we open ourselves to a wisdom from outside of ourselves, a wisdom that takes into account more than our personal well-being, we can grow into creative and holy human beings. The fact that something helps us or hurts us ceases to be the dominant factor as we judge right from wrong, or good from bad. The center of our concern moves from our own egos to the world which God has called us to love as we receive His Word into our hearts. The Word of God is truly a healing word.

In both praising God and receiving His Word at Eucharist, God can also transform us in another way, to the degree to which we are open to it. If we have consciously chosen to meet God in this community form of worship, He is also able to penetrate those attitudes that separate us from other human beings and keep us from experiencing the beauty and wonder in them.

Because of the influence of psychology on our culture, we have developed a heightened sense of individuality and person-hood. When this heightened sense of self is combined with selfishness, however, this generally positive development turns negative. It causes us not only to live for ourselves but also to live separately from others, not relating with them, caring about them, or working with them. We have seen the effects of this way of living in our neighborhoods and our churches, in our politics and our play, and, often most distressingly, in our families: being concerned first for "number one," for ourselves alone. This attitude is personalism in a decadent form.

While biblical principles encourage each of us to become all that we were created to be, the Bible does not encourage this kind of personalism. And yet we must face the fact that, because we have grown up in this society, and whether or not we agree with this value system, it is a part of our lives. Furthermore, it affects many people's attitudes about community worship.

They would rather be left alone in their worship, so that they can develop a personal relationship with God.

But the truth is that God calls us to worship together, and He does not ask this of us simply for the sake of convenience. In other words, it is not just that there are too many lay people for each to have his or her own private Eucharistic celebration that brings us together for worship. Rather, community is an essential part of Eucharist.

The Eucharist is God's sign of His unconditional affection for us. It is the celebration of His victory over all that is destructive in this world. As such, it confronts all that would destroy or mutilate our human natures as He created them to be. Through Eucharist, our isolationism, privatism, fear of people who are different from ourselves, and the loneliness that comes from all of these are themselves destroyed, for they bring psychological and spiritual death. Through Eucharistic celebration we come to know that we do not have to live in emotional prisons of mistrust and fear.

Again, we know that those reactions that separate us from other people are common human experiences, but again we know that they are not the best kind. They are a sign that we need yet to be humanized, for these attitudes prevent us from achieving our fullest human potential as persons and as Christians.

I am aware of a small group of Christians who for years have been meeting informally to share prayer, praise, and the work of God in their daily lives. At one point in their history, however, they became divided by theological differences so severely that the group split in two, with both factions losing members in their separate meetings. Their parish priest, seeking to minister to them in their difficulty, invited both groups and all former members to celebrate Eucharist with him once a month for healing and reconciliation. As they reflected on God's Word calling them to forgive each other, they allowed themselves to be drawn together in community again. God began to bind their wounds and then to bind them to each other through sharing Eucharist. Today they are a greater sign than ever before of God's power to bring people together through Eucharist, the Sacrament of unity.

As we celebrate Eucharist with God's people in community, God begins to dwell in those parts of us that are stunting our emotional and spiritual growth, to the degree to which we are open to His doing so. We express our openness by participating with others in the songs, words, and actions which the ceremony calls from us. And as we do so, God is able to begin transforming and healing these weaknesses in us, to begin humanizing us.

It is difficult for many people, especially Americans brought up on tales of the "pioneer spirit," and especially men who are often unconsciously educated from youth to think they should be self-sufficient, to see that it is a weakness to be a person who does not want to reveal self to others, a person who keeps to him- or herself and wants others to do the same. And yet it is true by definition—simply because it is impossible to be self-sufficient. It is when we do not acknowledge our need for others that we often find we need them the most. It is built into our human natures. We are simply created that way.

God's work of transformation and renewal through His Word happens more quickly and painlessly, of course, if we choose consciously to be confronted with our unwholeness and allow God to change us. At first it may not be easy to participate in community worship, but our enthusiasm for it will grow as we are faithful to God's call to us. For in drawing more deeply into community worship, we are drawing more deeply into the Body of Christ, through which God can perform in us miracles of power and love. Only as we enter the Body of Christ and secure ourselves in that spiritual union with others will we be able to answer God's call to be Christ on earth. None of us on our own could begin to imitate the breadth and depth of Christ's love, but together we can, as we are filled with His Spirit.

The great work of Christ we must imitate is the self-sacrifice of His life in love for others, and He indeed prepares us for this ministry as we worship in community. Praising God and receiving His Word as the Body of Christ, however, as much a sacrifice as these have been, are merely preparing us for the greater self-sacrifice He will ask of us next, the one that will ask us for all and give us all in return.

four

A SACRIFICE OF SELF

Having received greater insight into our human situation through praising God and receiving His Word, we are ready to enter the heart of Eucharistic worship, the sacrifice of ourselves to God. The means we use to sacrifice are symbolic: bread and wine. We shall investigate the long tradition they have in the history of mankind as symbols of human life. But the focus of our interest shall be the meaning of sacrifice itself.

The center of the mystery of the Eucharist is based on Jesus' simple, incontrovertible words recorded similarly in Mark, Matthew and Luke (cf. Mt 26:26-28 and Lk 22:19-20):

> And as they were eating he took some bread, and when he had said the blessing he broke it and gave it to them. "Take it," he said, "this is my body." Then he took a cup (of wine), and when he had returned thanks he gave it to them, and all drank from it, and he said to them, "This is my blood, the blood of the covenant, which is to be poured out for many" (Mk 14:22-24).

Jesus transforms bread and wine into His own Body and Blood; nothing in the text will let us avoid this fact. In making the bread and wine of the Passover His own Person, Jesus begins a new tradition of remembering the power of God Who saves people from evil. For the Jews up to that time and now, Passover brought them into the experience of the first band of Israelites who walked away from Pharaoh's despotism under the power of Yahweh and the leadership of Moses. For the followers of Jesus from that point on, this new celebration of Passover would bring them into both the presence and the Person of the living Lord Jesus Christ, Who freed all peoples from every force both within and without that would keep us from wholeness and holiness.

The entire meaning of Eucharist, then, depends on our keeping in mind what we have said about "remembering" in Chapter 2—namely, that when Jesus said, "Do this in memory of me" (Lk 22:19), or "Do this as a memorial of me," or "Do this in commemoration of me," what He meant was not that we recall the events of His life and what a wonderful person He was whenever we celebrate the Lord's Supper, but that through this celebration we *enter into* Him and His life.

Therefore, the heart of the mystery of Eucharist is this: *As the bread and wine are transformed and made sacred, so are we transformed and made sacred, if we unite ourselves consciously and prayerfully with these symbols of the sacrifice.* To understand what this statement means, however, we need to investigate both the meaning of the *symbols* we use and the meaning of *sacrifice* itself.

The bread and wine are our sacrifice to God. For our sacrifice to become a self-sacrifice, however, we must allow these elements to represent us. But how can we unite ourselves with inanimate elements? What would call us to them, or them to us?

The basis of the unity that human beings can have with inanimate objects is the fact that our minds can see in objects outside of themselves qualities or attributes that represent human life or the human personality. In a word, it is the ability to make symbols. For example, we can see in a stone a symbol of the hardness of the human heart, in a flower bud a symbol of new psychological or spiritual life.

We need and use many symbols, all with different meanings and purposes, and all with different degrees of power. The power of a symbol depends on its universality—in other words, the less universally applicable a symbol is, the less power it can have on our minds. For example, a preacher can hold high a one dollar bill in the midst of a sermon and it could be a good symbol of greed, but that would be most true in the United States of America. In a European country, the dollar bill would probably be recognized, but people would identify with it less; and in the outposts of a third world country far away from cities and commerce, people may have no idea what a dollar bill is at all.

Bread and wine do not fit into this category of "limited symbols" because they are common to all cultures. Every culture can identify them and identify with them. Furthermore, as Jung says, they are "natural symbols"—in other words, they need no verbal explanation, for intuitively all people know what they mean (pp. 252-254), although a few words here may help us to make our understanding of them more conscious.

Because they are from the earth, they are symbolic of our earthly natures; because they are products of work, they are symbolic of human labor; because they are the products of civilization (to make bread and wine people first needed to stop wandering as nomads and settle in one place where they could grow wheat and grapes), they are symbolic of those human virtues that make human civilization possible; because they are a great achievement, they are symbolic of mankind's industry, patience, devotion, care, and knowledge, all of which are necessary for such an achievement; and because they participate in the annual cycle of death and rebirth in nature, they are symbolic of our spiritual death and resurrection.

And besides being natural symbols of human life and culture, they are also natural symbols of our human natures.

Bread (natural, whole grain bread) has most of the nutrients human beings need to sustain physical life. It is a basic means of physical sustenance all the world over. It therefore is a natural symbol of our *physical selves*. Wine completes the nutritional balance human beings need, but, more importantly, it has a relationship to our inner selves. God has made wine "to make (people) cheerful" (Ps 104:15). The ancients thought wine contained spirits, and when people drank wine, they began to act differently than they did before imbibing it because the spirits in the wine were acting through them. So wine has always been seen as "inspiriting," and therefore it is a natural symbol of our interior beings, our *psychological and spiritual selves*.

In the depth of ourselves, then, we respond to bread and wine, even though we may sometimes find these responses difficult to discover consciously. Our difficulty arises from the fact that most of us are physically distant from the growing of wheat and grapes and the production of bread and wine. However, they are apt symbols of our sacrifice of self to God because we respond so universally to them, even if we do so somewhat unconsciously. Furthermore, we can see that it would be impossible to sacrifice ourselves to God using only words and not using some physical symbols, because no amount of words could ever fully describe us as we are. These particular symbols are necessary because they are able to sum up the complicated physical, psychological, and spiritual situation of human and divine life that we live.

Bread and wine are symbols of the sacrifice, and they represent our entire lives. But now we must ask what it means to sacrifice.

When we sacrifice we are giving away something that belongs to us without expecting anything in return. This is the reason, for example, that when the ancients sacrificed an object to their gods, they burned it, or threw it down a hole, or threw it into the water. By doing this they could not receive any good from the object again, and thus not be accused of not sacrificing it at all.

In this sense, a sacrifice is technically different from a gift or a present, for which in most social situations we can expect a return gift. A sacrifice comes from a deeper love and commitment, and it expresses the true intentions of the heart. The kind of sacrifice, the meaning the object of sacrifice has to the person giving it, and the abandon (or lack thereof) with which it is given all express and reveal the true nature of the person making the sacrifice.

What the ancients did in sacrificing to their gods was a dim prefiguring of the complete sacrifice God has always wanted from human beings, which He has revealed through Jesus— namely, the sacrifice of ourselves. The ancients gave their gods objects of worth and value with which they identified and which had great meaning for them. Destroying these objects expressed the respect or love or admiration they had for their gods. Sacrificing them was like giving a part of their hearts away. It was probably from the emotional impact of sacrifice that the terrible practice of human sacrifice came to be. Total respect or love demanded a total sacrifice, that is, giving away the most precious possession one could have—a child, for instance. We can see how the desire and need to give himself totally to his God was not unknown to Abraham, also, for when Yahweh asked him to sacrifice his first-born and only son, Isaac, he did not flinch, but accepted Yahweh's request as a valid one (Gn 22:1-10).

What God wanted from Abraham, however, was not the life of his son, but, in a certain sense, his own life. God wanted Abraham's heart. He wanted Abraham to find the meaning and security of his life not in his child—a way people of all ages have found these psychological necessities—but in Him alone. God wanted Abraham freely to give his heart to Him and to have faith in Him—that is, to have a unique, personal relationship in which he would yield the very center of his being to God. So we can say that God was seeking from Abraham a different kind of human sacrifice, a kind that was symbolized by the life of his son.

Our hearts are the most natural symbols to us of our truest selves, as when we say we have given someone our heart in love. We must also consider our hearts a kind of possession, because we cannot "give" what we do not own or have. Similarly, we see our lives as our own possessions, as in the statement, "It's my life and I'll do with it what I want." And it is precisely from this feeling of ownership of our hearts and our lives that ethical questions arise for each of us: What is the best, right, most appropriate thing to do with my heart, with my life? To whom do I give them, or do I keep them for myself?

Jung reports that the identification that human beings make with things they own was first described in psychological detail by Lévy-Bruhl in his study of tribal cultures. He noticed that when a tribesman, for example, spoke of his own canoe as opposed to another man's canoe, he put a suffix on the end of the word that denoted animation or aliveness. Thus he called this phenomenon the *participation mystique*, because the object seemed to participate in the life of the owner, and the owner in the life of the object. Jung goes on to say that this *participation mystique* functions through our unconscious. In other words, the unknown in us (unconsciousness) reaches out and contacts the unknown in the object (all objects are partially unknown, for we could never know everything there is to know about them) and creates a oneness with it (pp. 255-256).

What is important to realize is that when we identify with an object and perceive it as ours, it begins to matter to us what happens to it, simply because it becomes attached to our egos. It has become, unconsciously, a symbol of ourselves, and so we see it as a part of our personalities. Thus we are setting the stage for something dark to occur. As Jung says:

When, therefore, I give away something that is "mine," what I am giving is essentially a symbol, a thing of many meanings; but, owing to my unconsciousness of its symbolic character, it adheres to my ego, because it is part of my personality. Hence there is, explicitly or implicitly, a personal claim bound up with every gift. There is always an unspoken "give that thou mayest receive." Consequently the gift always carries with it a personal intention, for the mere giving of it is not a sacrifice. It only becomes a sacrifice if I give up the implied intention of receiving something in return. If it is to be a true sacrifice, the gift must be given as if it were being destroyed. Only then it is possible for the egoistic claim to be given up (pp. 256-257).

This expectation of a return gift is the dark attitude that comes from the unconscious when the *participation mystique* is at work. It is our way of saying that we care what happens to this "gift" because we do not see it as separate from our egos. When we are unaware of the various things, within and without, to which our egos become attached, we know that the *participation mystique* is operative in us. And when we are even unconscious of when and how it is operative (and it is always at work in us) we can make no sacrifice to God. For in our unconsciousness, we have no knowledge of which things in our lives have meaning for us and therefore would symbolize our hearts or our lives. We have no knowledge of which things in our lives are worthy of sacrifice because we do not know how deeply we are attached to them. We cannot make a worthy sacrifice if that which we are giving to God has no conscious value or meaning to us. So it is important that we become conscious of the possessions we consider important in life.

Those possessions could be many, and they are not all

necessarily material. For example, we can become attached to power, intelligence, talent, spiritual gifts, position, authority, or the opposite of any of these, as well as to material things. Possessions help us create the self-image we need. It matters little whether our need is to see ourselves bigger or smaller, more important or less important than we are. Through the *participation mystique* which operates unconsciously, these possessions are creating a fantasy of strength or weakness upon which our egos depend. We need them either for our self-esteem (when our fantasy is strength) or to sustain neurotic, self-righteous, or otherwise irresponsible thought-behavior patterns (when our fantasy is weakness). What does make the difference is that we realize our dependency on them, and that we sacrifice both our possessions and our dependency to God.

But even after we give our gift to God, it is not a sacrifice if we are expecting something in return. Many times we sacrifice to God thinking we are buying His love or forgiveness for our sin. At other times the return gift we want is the feeling of moral satisfaction that we have indeed done what we should have—made a proper sacrifice to the Almighty. Or maybe we are doing all of this to obtain some special favor from God (not that we should not look to God to do good things for us, but He acts on our behalf as a free gift of love, not because we have sacrificed to Him). In any case, our sacrifice is not totally real, since we cannot truly be giving something away freely and simultaneously be expecting something in return.

So, as we look at the real meaning of sacrifice, we find ourselves coming to a difficult conclusion: Celebrating Eucharist means being poor. It means giving our lives as a gift and not receiving any "thing" back but a relationship. It means facing the poverty of our humanity—the fact that we are no more or no less than we are. It means allowing the *participation mystique* to be broken, so that we see ourselves simply as we are, with nothing masking or hiding our true natures. In this sense, poverty is a call to all Christians. "How happy are the poor in spirit; theirs is the kingdom of heaven" (Mt 5:3). Those who freely, happily, and especially consciously choose a life of evangelical poverty are a witness to all of us to help us know and love ourselves, for they have chosen to depend on less and less to prop up their egos and keep themselves from realizing the basic truth of human existence that we come into this world with nothing, and we leave it with nothing.

The Sacrament of the Lord's Supper encourages us into this kind of spiritual poverty through continuous sacrifice of our selfishness. When we continue to sacrifice more and more of ourselves and our lives to God, we begin to curb our desire for and need of things (not necessarily material) which fill our egos by adhering to them through the *participation mystique* and make us self-centered people. Freed of our dependency on things we are empty, and in our emptiness we can thirst for God alone, as the psalmist did:

> As a doe longs
>   for running streams
> so longs my soul
>   for you, my God.
> My soul thirsts for God,
>   the God of life;
> when shall I go to see
>   the face of God? (Ps 42:1-2)

The fulfillment of Eucharistic sacrifice is to desire God alone. We do receive when we sacrifice to God, but it is not a "thing" that is ours, for God gives us Himself, and we cannot possess Him. In a real sense this gift possesses us, it takes us out of control. Having given everything to Him, our inner selves are empty, and yet needing something to adhere to, they adhere to Christ. The goal of Eucharistic celebration is to effect in us a *participation mystique* with Christ! The goal is to empty all the parts of our lives of our attachment to them so that they can be filled with Christ and transformed. The goal is to see Him as the only one Who gives us true meaning and security—because He is. The goal is to identify with Him, and so become as loving, forgiving, caring, hoping, believing, and enduring as He is.

But when we identify with Christ in this way and He makes us like Himself, we are faced with a dilemma. We want to be this way, but we also fear being this way, because we know that these virtues place great demands on us, and because we know that we cannot sustain them.

Our fear is real because we indeed are incapable of maintaining those attitudes in our hearts if we are unassisted by a power greater than ourselves. But if we identify with God and we have emptied ourselves of all else so that there is room for the infinite God, He will be living in us, and He will do the work. This is essentially that same reality about which Christians have written for centuries—that deep union of a human soul with Christ that can only be called mystical. This is a process that happens in stages and degrees, and it is able to be propelled by every self-sacrifice we make through Eucharist.

As we take an overview of all we have discovered to this point about sacrifice, we can see that sacrificing ourselves creates two complementary but divergent movements in our lives. As Jung says:

> Ordinary giving for which no return is expected is felt as a loss; but a sacrifice is meant to be like a loss, so that one may be sure that the egoistic claim (for a return gift) no longer exists. Therefore the gift should be given as if it were being destroyed. But since the gift represents myself, I have in that case destroyed myself, given myself away without expectation of return. Yet, looked at in another way, this

intentional loss is also a gain, for if you can give
yourself it proves that you possess yourself. Nobody
can give what he has not got (p. 257).

Therefore, self-sacrifice is a two-sided reality. At first of
course, it means giving ourselves as a gift to another, and that is
tantamount to a kind of self-destruction. Surely this can be
counted as a loss. But since we cannot give what we do not have,
we must have "possessed" ourselves or "found" ourselves if we
have been able to give ourselves as a gift. In other words, we
must become more conscious of the persons we truly are if we
are the objects of our own sacrifice. Surely this must be counted
as a gain.

Making a sacrifice of ourselves, then, implies considerable
self-knowledge. The Eucharist challenges us to "find" and
"own" the entirety of ourselves—even and especially those
parts of ourselves of which we are unconscious, whether or not
we approve or disapprove of them. Eucharist gives us the
opportunity to "reassemble" all the parts of ourselves—that is,
to find those "lost" parts of our personalities, those parts of
ourselves to which we have chosen not to attend because they
are weak or ugly or too threatening to our conscious egos. Thus
through Eucharist we bring them into consciousness and sacrifice them to God. Self-sacrifice is "losing our lives in order to
save them" (Mt 10:39) and, in moving us in this direction, it
moves us to imitate Christ and be one with Him. The process of
humanization thus leads to spirituality.

Self-sacrifice also demands from us the awareness of how
deeply we are attached to the things in our lives. It challenges us
to admit our dependency on things and let go of them. It
challenges us to depend ultimately on God alone. How grateful
we need to become for that challenge, for in reality, at the end of
our lives we will not be able to depend on anything or anyone
but God and His love. Eucharist is preparing us to meet God
face-to-face with dignity.

As we describe self-sacrifice in its most conscious form, we see clearly that it is what Jesus did with His life and in His death. He loved every aspect of His humanity and gave all to His Father for His work and glory. He let go of everything that would keep Him from depending on God alone for His security and for the meaning of His life. He expressed these attitudes in word and action every day of His life. The recorded accounts of His public ministry—when the pressures toward selfishness would have been greater than at any other time, precisely because of the demands people made of Him in ministry—attest to His unswerving dedication to living life according to these principles. His death was the culmination and peak experience of these principles, for under unimaginable pressure to do something for Himself, He continued to live a life of self-sacrifice to the very end.

The Sacrament of the Lord's Supper is the continuation of His self-sacrifice. At the Last Supper Jesus sacrificed Himself to His Father, in communal love with His friends, in a symbolic and real way, in the moment of calm before the storm. Then He proceeded to live the exact meaning of what He had said and done with bread and wine. As every sacrifice needs an offering and someone to offer it—a victim and a priest—so Jesus was both victim and priest as He sacrificed His own life, both at the Last Supper and on the Cross.

At the Eucharistic celebration, the Sacrament of the Lord's Supper, Jesus continues to be the victim and the priest. The celebrant of Eucharistic worship is Jesus' minister, speaking and acting in His name. Jesus, the Eternal High Priest, continues to sacrifice Himself in this way through every Eucharistic celebration.

At each Eucharist, then, Jesus calls us to celebrate with Him. He calls us to sacrifice ourselves with Him, as He says to each of us, "Do this in memory of Me." He asks us to become conscious of various parts of ourselves we have not yet given to the Father, and to sacrifice them to Him. He asks us to become aware of how much we depend on things to make us feel good about ourselves and to give security and meaning to our lives, and He asks us with Him to give our dependency to the Father, finally relying on Him for the dignity, security, and meaning of our lives. He asks us to put on His mind (1 Cor 2:16) and to look at our lives from his point of view, to value that which truly has meaning, and to forego all that is of fading glory. Then He can offer to us the true glory that the Father offered to Him, for when we join in His sacrifice with all that is in us, we open ourselves to the Father's ability to transform human life, just as He did.

For Jesus was transformed, was raised from the dead, because of the perfect way He offered His life to His Father. On Easter morning all that had looked and felt like suffering, death, hopelessness, and despair was revealed as joy, life, hope, and the continuing promise of renewal.

In every Eucharistic celebration, Jesus offers the same opportunity for transformation and renewal to us in every part of our lives that we choose to sacrifice with Him to our Father. As we unite, through prayer and intentionality, our physical selves with the bread and our psychological and spiritual selves with the wine, we join in the dynamic movement of true sacrifice. We are made more whole, to praise our Father now with a fuller life, and preparing ourselves for our future resurrection from the dead.

The transformation, wholeness, healing, and renewal which are the result in us of Eucharistic sacrifice do not happen, then, because God is returning a gift to us in recognition of our gift to Him. Rather, they are the natural result of the dynamic of self-sacrifice. For sacrificing our egos creates an emptiness that needs to be filled, a motion toward the one to whom the sacrifice is made. In other words, it creates a love which in a small way restores that primal state of friendship between human beings and God before the Fall. That part of us which we have freely sacrificed to God enters into the heart of God Himself, or, as Jesus described it, it enters into God's Kingdom—a phrase which describes a relationship with God in which He is master and ruler. And where God reigns, there is wholeness, holiness, and hope.

In Eucharistic celebration and sacrifice Jesus continues to give Himself to the Father, for that is His eternal stance before Him, and He leads us and guides us to do the same. Although we do not now have the kind of consciousness He has by which we can give ourselves completely to the Father, Jesus teaches us how to move toward that goal by sacrificing parts of ourselves and parts of our lives to the Father in each Eucharistic celebration. In this way we become a human sacrifice to God, bloodless because we sacrifice ourselves through the symbols of bread and wine with which we have closely identified ourselves, and more efficacious because it is the truest sacrifice of our hearts and lives we can make. It has the power of Abraham's sacrifice of Isaac, or of Jesus' sacrifice in Gethsemani.

Our sacrifice, indeed, becomes more real because we are giving what means most to us—control over our own lives. Jesus, Who lives in us through Baptism and Christian virtue, sacrifices our selfishness to God. All sacrifice is necessarily painful, and this kind of sacrifice could, in a psychological and spiritual sense, be the most painful. But it is the only way to redeem these parts of ourselves and our lives. They are uncon-scious and lost to us, or we are unconsciously attached to them and they are destroying us. In either case our relationship with them needs to be brought into the light.

When we sacrifice these parts of us, they are released from the darkness of our unconscious (the *participation mystique*) and they become conscious. In this way, the Christ Who lives within becomes freer, more alive, more able to do His work in us and through us in this world. Thus the processes of humanization and spirituality merge in Eucharistic sacrifice. Then, once we have made our human self-sacrifice and united it with Christ's, we are prepared for the culmination of this celebration, the mystery of mysteries: We are prepared for union with God Himself.

five

A UNION OF HEARTS

We saw in Chapter 4 that the dynamic of true self-sacrifice creates a movement toward the one to whom the sacrifice is made. As we have come to understand what it means to sacrifice ourselves to God in Eucharist, we have seen that self-sacrifice reestablishes that friendship between human beings and God which was first broken in the Fall of mankind in Eden. Our Eucharistic celebration, then, propels us into a deep union with Jesus, the culmination of which is Holy Communion.

But the Jesus with Whom Eucharist unites us is a God Who in Gethsemani selflessly prepared for His freely chosen immolation on the Cross. If we are to be one with Him in Communion, then, in a very real sense our union needs to be established from the beginning of the celebration through the common purpose of self-sacrifice—that is, we need to be as ready and willing to sacrifice ourselves to God as Jesus is.

The consequences of this fact are obvious: To the degree that our purpose is not the same as Jesus' the effectiveness of our sacrifice is limited. For this attitude of giving to the utmost which we call self-sacrifice is the most godly attitude to which we can aspire, and so it is the only attitude that can adequately prepare us for that complete union with His heart we call Communion.

Communion without this attitude, furthermore, can become a lie that we tell with actions as well as with words, and so it can be dangerous to our personal integrity. When we receive Communion we are eating of the sacrifice; this is a custom that dates back to ancient times in the Jewish religion, in which it expressed the involvement of the community in the sacrifice as well as their agreement to the terms of the covenant which the sacrifice was creating, as when the Jewish people ate of the lamb of Passover promising to obey the Mosaic Law. When we consume the bread and wine of Communion we are attesting to our assent to the sacrifice of Jesus, saying that we are willing to live as He lives, totally dedicated to the Father and His values, and totally sacrificing ourselves for others.

To the degree to which we are intending to live in deep relationship with Christ, then, we will also then be willing to come into union with others, simply because that is the way He lives. Union with Jesus that excludes others in whom He finds His identity (the Body of Christ) is no union at all. Only by choosing to be like Jesus do we receive Communion with integrity. Communion is therefore not only a relationship with the Divine but also with the human, all on the spiritual plane. This spiritual union with Christ and others is what it means to be the Body of Christ, and Communion is one important way Jesus creates His Body on earth. To deny this dimension of Communion is to deny the nature of the experience itself.

As we pray over the bread and wine in the Eucharistic Prayer and in the Words of Institution, they become the Body and Blood of Jesus. Thus Jesus continues His eternal self-sacrifice to His Father in every Eucharistic celebration because He continues to have the same perfect attitude of love for us and for His Father that impelled Him first to sacrifice His life on Calvary.

Now, however, He draws us into that same perfect attitude and the same transformation that results from it. If we have become conscious of ourselves through the preceding parts of the ceremony, and if we have also consciously united ourselves with the bread and wine so that as Jesus again offers Himself to the Father He is offering us as well, we are drawn into that transformation. For when the bread and wine become Jesus, what has been united to the bread and wine enters into Jesus' heart. There he can make us like Himself for we have emptied ourselves of our own plans for our lives in the act of self-sacrifice.

Furthermore, because Jesus' love for His Father was perfectly expressed in the freely chosen sacrifice of His life, He is perfectly one with the Father. And, if we are in Jesus' heart, so are we in the Father's heart. The gift of ourselves has become completely acceptable to Him because Jesus has carried it there. Our Father receives the sacrifice of our lives because it is united with Jesus' fully conscious and perfect sacrifice of His life. Our Father is pleased that we are trying to imitate His Son by becoming conscious of ourselves and sacrificing ourselves to Him, and so becoming humanized. For only in the heart of God is this complete transformation, healing, and renewal possible.

It is because this dynamic is at work that we can pray in faith just before receiving Communion, "Lord, I am not worthy that you should come into me; say but the word and I will be healed." In union with the humble attitude of the centurion whose story is told in the eighth chapter of Matthew's Gospel, we trust God to do a mighty work for which we have yet seen little or no evidence. Our prayer expresses our belief that, because we now rest in the heart of God Himself, we are assured that this loving and powerful God will be motivated by His love to use His power for us. Our prayer also expresses an expectation of results specifically from this Eucharist—that because of it we will see the effects of God's healing and renewal in our lives. We can expect God to work on our behalf because we are in intimate relationship with Him through self-sacrifice which draws us into God as nothing else can, and we are looking forward in a few moments to fulfill that relationship totally in deep oneness—communion—with Him.

God wanted to be intimate with human beings from the

beginning. The fact that Yahweh walked in the garden in the cool of the day looking for Adam and Eve (Gn 3:8) implies that He wanted to be on warm and intimate terms with them. When human beings rejected God's offer, however, God would not be stopped, and He has found another way for us to be close to Him. He has provided us with an access to His heart through His Son Jesus and the Sacrament we call Eucharist. This intimacy is His greatest desire and our greatest need. Since we live in a society preoccupied with "doing," we need our God to call us to that quality of relationship by which we discover that we are much more than consumers and producers of goods, but that we have value and worth intrinsic to our very natures.

From God's heart emanates all that is good, and so as we rest in His heart in Holy Communion, we are consumed by Him, filled with Him, revitalized in Him, if we have come to this point aware of what we are doing. As we have sacrificed to Him in the first parts of the celebration we are now filled with Him, because we have emptied ourselves of all desires other than to be close to Him.

As we are filled with God, we can be nothing but filled with new life—that is, revitalized, renewed, transformed, healed, and humanized. For we are at the origin of our human natures when we are in our Father's heart, and He knows what we need, what we seek, and what we are capable of doing. Also when we freely choose to receive Holy Communion, we are saying that we will be responsible for the life (grace) He gives us.

Communion is that union of our hearts with God's that brings His life to fulfillment in us. This can be one of the most important and exciting events in our lives if we have come this far in consciousness, that is, if we are aware of what He intends for it to mean in our lives.

Many people, however, come to this point of the Eucharistic celebration relatively unconscious of the purpose of the event. Maybe all they think has happened is that they have spent some time worshiping God and now He wants to spend some time with them. They know that Communion is, or at least should be, an intensely spiritual and uplifting moment in their lives, but they cannot verbalize the reasons it should be so. Furthermore, for many people it has not been an exalted experience for quite some time, and they often wonder if the beauty of Communion when they were younger was related more to their youthful impressionability, or maybe to the careful preparation that led to, for example, First Communion Day.

Others may merely attend Eucharist out of a sense of duty or obligation. They often attend and do not participate fully primarily because they are following a principle they learned when they were young—that the right thing to do is to worship God once a week. Without making an adult decision about it, they go through a ritual of giving themselves to God because they were told when they were children that it was the right thing to do, and thus they are not psychologically and spiritually involved in what they are doing.

These attitudes entirely undercut the purpose that Eucharist is meant to have in our lives. This celebration, which is supposed to make us more aware of who we are so that we can be transformed more completely into the image of Christ, under the influence of any of these attitudes, becomes a means of remaining unconscious and of not growing psychologically or spiritually. For when we are in the grip of these notions we are participating in the Lord's Supper only "going through the motions," sacrificing ourselves to God because it seems like "the proper thing to do."

To sacrifice ourselves to God means we give ourselves to Him expecting nothing in return. But, as Jung says from a psychological point of view, when we sacrifice by rote because it is the proper thing we already have a return gift for our sacrifice—a sense of moral satisfaction that we have done what is right (p. 260). To be sure, our return gift is as shallow as our original offering, but it is still there. And being filled with our own righteousness we have no room for the expansiveness of God. Indeed, we feel no need for Him because we feel perfectly fine just the way we are. Of course, we will still need Him to do those favors for us that are humanly impossible for us to do alone. But we have no room for Him in the fabric of our lives, and we see no need to go through all the effort it takes to become His friend. We have retained our selfishness, and our lives and egos remain narrow, unable to be transformed.

But, as Jung continues, if we give ourselves to God, renouncing our claim on a return gift for inner reasons; if we sacrifice ourselves acknowledging the pain of giving up our right to have things our way; and if we acknowledge the pain of sacrificing ourselves to a relatively unknown God, placing our lives in His hands, for reasons that are even unclear to us, reasons against which we may even resist and rebel—then we are acknowledging the truthful ambiguity of life and of this situation. In this ambiguity we are left empty and therefore are ready for Him to fill us. But that infilling will have to be both a surprise and a gift. We cannot give ourselves to Him expecting it, or the sacrifice is not real. That would be expecting a return gift.

The pain of the emptiness quickly yields to the life that only He can create. With great earnestness, devotion, attention to detail, and feelings of piety, we can sacrifice ourselves to God because we see it is the proper thing to do, and all we will have is a sacrifice that *looks* real. In this case so much self-righteousness and self-consciousness fills our hearts that there is no room for God. But if we renounce our claim on a return gift for painful inner reasons often unclear even to us, while no satisfying feelings of moral accomplishment accompany it, what we have is the real thing. This was the nature of Abraham's intended sacrifice of Isaac, and of Jesus' decision in Gethsemani. Just as they were delivered from evil and transformed under the power of God, so will we.

In this way Eucharist becomes vital to our lives, all-encompassing, essential to our living, because it is expanding and humanizing our egos, allowing the best in us to be freed and expressed. Surely, no one who saw Eucharist in this way could find it boring.

There was a time in my life that I experienced in a rather dramatic way what we have discovered about self-sacrifice through Eucharist in this and the preceding chapters of this book. The sacrifice God required of me was my apostolate. It was one that I loved, and one in which I found deep meaning for my life. The precipitating factor for needing to sacrifice it was that the structure which supported it suddenly fell away, and so it looked as if I might have to begin an apostolate I did not like nor did I think was right for me, although no clear decisions had as yet been made.

The experience left me not only disappointed in a few people but also in a God on Whose help I had been depending to do a work I had thought He had wanted me to do for Him. I was confused, wondering whether the idea for the apostolate that had fallen apart was mine or His. I agonized with this question through sleepless nights and long hours of conversation with my spiritual director and friends.

My problem became all too clear. I knew I must sacrifice the lost apostolate to God, and not try to regain it by any political maneuvering. But I could not give it up simply or completely because it was too much a part of me (the *participation mystique* at work). I found myself giving the apostolate to God only because I knew that, if He wanted it taken from me, He would have whatever He wanted because He is all-powerful. I gave my life to Him, but then quickly added my expectations of how He should take care of me. I withdrew from Him the right to send me where He wanted me to work, instead telling Him what I was and was not ready to do. I knew my attitude was much like that of a little child afraid of an angry father, but I could not progress much further on my own.

Then I attended a conference at which I talked with some friends who told me what I needed to hear—I had to give my apostolate to God because I loved Him, not because I was afraid of Him. And so it was to a Eucharistic celebration that I came with this resolution in my heart.

I celebrated the Eucharist as I have been describing it in this and the preceding chapters, giving my life and apostolate to God, with great effort focusing on Him first and on what I wanted second, and not even suggesting to Him what I thought the outcome in my life should be. At the beginning of the celebration I praised God, not with joy, I must admit, but with dedication. I received each reading from Scripture openly, and there was a message in each one of them that helped me a little more to let go of the apostolate I loved. Prayerfully I united the labor of my apostolate with the bread and all my love for and attachment to it with the wine, and I prayed that it all would be taken into the heart of Jesus for His transforming miracle to happen, first in my heart. My prayer left me feeling empty and frightened.

When I received the Body and Blood of Jesus, I believed with everything available in me that God was transforming me by purifying me of my attachments to the apostolate. Upon returning from Communion I saw a scene that touched me in the depth of my being—a participant at our conference who had bone cancer sitting in a chair with his wife kneeling at his feet, her arms wrapped around his waist. Everything in me broke free and my last attachment to the apostolate I so loved was shattered as I said to myself, "If they can live in faith in their situation, I can live in faith in whatever situation may come my way." Finally, the apostolate was no longer "mine" in my heart.

Jesus had broken through my attachments to create a *participation mystique* directly between His heart and mine.

I was free to find the new direction in which God was leading my life. It came in a few days, and to my surprise it was neither the apostolate I so loved nor the one I had feared would be forced upon me. God sent me on a new mission in which He blessed me with all I could ever hope for. The personal freedom and faith that came from that Eucharist was the result of His love breaking my unconscious clinging to a thing in which I had found great security, and filling me with a clinging to Him.

Eucharist brings us into an experience of love that frees us from needing anything else. That sounds wonderful as an idea, but when it becomes a possibility and then a reality in our lives, we find how fearsome it is to be in the hands of an all-loving God. Eucharist prepares us little by little for the experience of being in God's hands as we know it in this life, and as we will know it in the next. For someday each of us will have to face the reality which Eucharist is gently and persistently asking us to admit—namely, that all we have for security in this life is God alone. Every other security is an illusion. In Eucharist we come to know that love which is strong enough to be our security in every situation. From the experience of His love as we rest in His heart, we learn to love and we find out that to love is the most perfect attitude, for it guides us into the selflessness that makes us whole and holy.

six

EUCHARIST CAN BE LIFE-CHANGING

Many of us were taught as children that every day we should give our lives to God, because we are made in His image and likeness, and because we are made to know Him, love Him, and serve Him in this world and to be happy with Him in the next. Offering our lives to Him was the means through which we know, love, and serve God, and so it was an important thing to do. We were supposed to do it every morning in our prayers and every time we celebrated the Lord's Supper.

These are all ideas with which we would never want to argue. The only difficulty was that many of us found that we could not do it. We knew we should, we may have even been completely convinced it was a good idea, that it made sense, but we could not in fact ever give our lives to God. We did not even know who we were or what our lives were about. We were not conscious of what we were offering.

Our difficulties are not unusual. Psychologists tell us that most people are relatively unconscious of themselves and their lives, and they estimate that about 90% of our lives is unconscious to most of us. The fact is that our lives are too big a reality for us to be giving them to God all at one time, except in a ceremonial sense. We cannot be conscious of our entire selves or our entire lives at one moment, so we cannot literally sacrifice our lives to God in any real way.

When people say they have given their lives to God, what

they usually mean is that at one time in their lives they prayed *intending* to give their lives to God, and now day-by-day they are finding out what that means. Even if a person were to consider the notion of complete self-sacrifice from many different points of view, taking due amount of time and energy to do so, he or she would still have to find out what it means to give a life to God experientially. After all, our lives are, in a real sense, all we have, and intending to give them as a gift creates certain dynamics of resistance and grace with which a person must cope on a day-to-day basis.

The fact is that we cannot give something to God if we are not aware of having it, and few people are aware of more than 10% of themselves at any given time. It is only this 10%, or some new factor that may rise up from the unconscious, that we can be giving to God. And who among us could even keep in his or her mind at the same time all of that 10%—simultaneously to be aware of our familial, social, and work-related roles in all their complexities of relationship, along with our gifts and talents, our weaknesses, our history, our preferences and choices, etc.? If awareness is the key to true self-sacrifice, we are all in a difficulty, because total awareness of ourselves is impossible, therefore making total self-sacrifice impossible.

But if we cannot bring ourselves to God in self-sacrifice, how can we give ourselves to God as we know we should? The answer to that question seems obvious, once we look at it: We can be aware of a *part of ourselves* and give *it* to God in self-sacrifice. The result is that we do give ourselves completely to God, but part-by-part, as it were. We do not set the impossible goal of sacrificing ourselves all at once, for that goal would necessitate being conscious of ourselves totally, and that is a state only Jesus has. As we become aware of more and more of ourselves, however, through our desire to sacrifice ourselves with Him to our Father, we expand our consciousness from 10% of our lives, and we begin to imitate Him.

To prepare ourselves for Eucharist, then, we need to

become aware of some element of our lives which we will sacrifice to God—some talent, quality, spiritual gift, personality characteristic, relationship, weakness, illness, goal, or undeveloped part of ourselves, and we give one part of ourselves to God each time we come to Him. Often the sacrifice we make to God on a particular day is determined by the most important goal we have at that time, or by the most pressing problem. Whatever it is, we bring it to God for transformation, healing, and renewal. Later we may develop in our love for God so that we come to the point of seeking through Eucharistic sacrifice to grow in virtue, spiritual giftedness, and zeal for the kingdom of God. But for now, all that is important is that we are sacrificing ourselves honestly and in consciousness.

If we are going to celebrate Eucharist for self-sacrifice, then, we will do best by determining a particular element of our lives we are going to give to God in each celebration. This part of our lives can be our "personal theme" for the Eucharist, and prayerfully and intentionally we bring this part of ourselves to God through each portion of it. The result is that this part of ourselves is transformed and brought into the Kingdom of God through conscious sacrifice and communion with God in love.

Let us then examine all of the parts of the Eucharistic celebration to see how their purpose is to help participants to be transformed and healed through sacrifice and communion, using as an example of our "personal theme" our work life, that is, our labor and its fruits in our lives.

Aware of our "personal theme" we begin the sacrament of the Lord's Supper by praising God in the Opening Rite, consisting of songs and prayers of praise and forgiveness. Often when we come before God we feel so unworthy that we want to leave all our humanness outside the church, as it were. But if we do that, we have nothing with which to praise Him. In actuality, we praise God best in our humanness and with our humanness. As St. Irenaeus (d. 203) said, "The glory of God is a human being fully alive." Therefore we praise Him with our work life uppermost in our minds. We do not praise Him in spite of it, but because of it, with it. In this Eucharist, it will be this part of us that will be praising Him the most. And is not this act a wonder? Maybe it is the first time that we have brought our labor and its fruits to kneel before God. It is precisely in moments like these that transformation begins, for praising God with this part of our lives brings it into relationship with Him, making it vulnerable to God and His action, open to all the good He can do for us.

In the Opening Rite we also ask God's forgiveness regarding any selfishness or other sinfulness in our lives pertinent to this "personal theme." We especially ask forgiveness for any desires we have for a return gift, for example, thinking that if we give our work life to Him He will bless us financially. We also ask to be forgiven for any way we desire that He acknowledge the gift we are giving. To the degree we can gain self-knowledge through this part of the celebration we will be free to relate with God in sacrifice and communion.

But self-knowledge is not easy, or even simple. Jesus suffered on the Cross to gain forgiveness for our sinfulness, but self-knowledge and humbly seeking His forgiveness is often the pain of the cross we must bear in life, the way we share in the sufferings of the Lord. As St. Paul expressed it, "All I want is to know Christ and the power of his resurrection and to share his sufferings by reproducing the pattern of his death" (Phil 3:10). We participate in the suffering of Christ by seeking forgiveness, and in His resurrection by being forgiven. Nothing can achieve transformation and wholeness in a finer way than the process of forgiveness. Maybe the reason that Jesus asked, pleaded, and often even demanded that we seek forgiveness, especially before we point out others' faults, is that doing so makes us conscious of who we truly are. Examination of our lives makes us conscious. Although this is a painful process it gives us the freedom to choose to seek forgiveness, and seeking forgiveness prepares us as nothing else can for self-sacrifice. As Jung explains:

...the integration or humanization of the self is initiated from the conscious side by our making ourselves aware of our selfish aims; we examine our motives and try to form as complete and objective a picture as possible of our own nature. It is an act of self-recollection, a gathering together of what is scattered, of all the things in us that have never been properly related, and a coming to terms with oneself with a view to achieving full consciousness. (Unconscious self-sacrifice is merely an accident, not a moral act) (p. 263).

After the Opening Rite we come to the first major part of the Eucharistic celebration, the Liturgy of the Word, comprising readings from the Bible, responses to the readings, and reflections on the readings, usually called a homily or sermon. We bring our "personal theme," our work life, to the Word of God. It is now enhanced from praising God with it and from insight that comes with seeking forgiveness. We listen to that Word, receiving it into our hearts, and allowing it further to make us conscious of what our labor and its fruits mean in our lives.

Remembering what we learned in Chapter 3, that the Bible is like no other book because it is alive with the presence of the Holy Spirit, we know that the Spirit of God can speak to our particular need, our "personal theme," through His Word. But we will not be able to hear Him unless we expect Him to speak. Therefore, as we bring to Him our work life or any other part of our lives, we keep this "personal theme" foremost in our minds and hearts as we hear the Word. We allow the Word to "rest upon" this issue in our lives which we are bringing to God, and we allow the Word to permeate it.

As the Word of God soaks into us like rain saturating the awaiting earth, the Spirit will be able to make us more conscious regarding this part of our lives. He will be able to speak to us

personally. We will receive in our hearts a word of encouragement, correction, wisdom, guidance, hope, or deeper insight
into our selfish claim on our own lives. But whatever we need
most will be there for us if we are expecting to hear it. A
Scripture passage written centuries ago and selected years ago
or selected for an entire congregation can and does have deep
personal meaning for those who await it openly.

Up to this point, the ceremony has been trying to help us
become more conscious of what it is we are sacrificing in our
lives. Praise, forgiveness, and receiving God's Word have
brought us to a deeper awareness of what our "personal
theme"—in this case, our work lives—means to us: the attachments we have to it, the resistance we have to its being transformed, and the hope we have for its renewal. Now we take this
heightened awareness and bring it to the Lord in sacrifice as we
enter the second major part of the celebration, the Liturgy of
the Eucharist.

We along with the celebrant prepare the gifts of bread and
wine. Through prayers and actions they are readied for sacrifice. But the sacrifice, from our personal point of view, is
incomplete if we have not joined ourselves to it. So we prayerfully and intentionally unite our "personal theme," in the case
of our example, our labor and its fruits, with the bread and wine
on the altar.

We unite the physical aspects of the situation (our labor
itself and the money we earn from it) with the bread, and the
emotional and spiritual aspects (our attachment to our work,
our feelings about it, the value we place on it, the value we place
on the money we earn from it) with the wine. We choose freely
to give them to God with Jesus, imitating Jesus, desiring to be
closer to Jesus. Thus the bread and wine become vehicles for
our sacrifice, symbols to which we all can relate in any circum-
stance no matter what we want to sacrifice to God.

After we prepare our gifts we pray over them and actually
sacrifice them to God. We do this in the prayer which in the

Roman Rite is called the Eucharistic Prayer, the Prayer of Thanksgiving. This is a prayer of blessing based on the Jewish *berakah*, in which we pray for the community and for ourselves. But most importantly in this prayer we *remember* God's saving deeds of old, and we ask the Spirit to descend upon the gifts of sacrifice and to unite them with God the Father.

In this sacred prayer our sacrifice becomes one with God. As we remember God's saving deed in the Word of Institution ("This is my body...this is my blood"), the sacrifice of whatever our "personal theme" represents becomes one with Jesus and enters His heart. In our example, our labor and its fruits enter Jesus' love in a special way. We believe that the physical aspects we united with the bread are renewed as the bread is changed into His Body, and that the emotional and spiritual aspects we united with the wine are renewed as the wine is changed into His Blood.

At this point the eternal nature of the one divine sacrifice is revealed as Jesus manifests Himself as both victim and priest of His own life, and, therefore, a window opens to the spiritual world. The rest of the Eucharistic Prayer expresses the unity we have with all the Church in the world today, as well as with the Church triumphant in heaven, again never letting us forget that Eucharist is a community endeavor, and helping us to see how the sacrifice we are making at this time in some way affects for the better the entire world. It releases into the universe the energy that comes from self-sacrifice.

We close the Eucharistic Prayer as well as this second major part of the celebration, the Liturgy of Eucharist, with a prayer called the Doxology, a word derived from the Greek word *doxa* which means "praise." It reads:

> Through Him, with Him, and in Him, in the unity of the Holy Spirit, all glory and honor is yours, Almighty Father, for ever and ever. Amen.

In this simple prayer, which is accompanied by a lifting of the sacred elements, the Body and Blood of Christ—a lifting that signifies a spiritualization of our gifts and an ascent to the Father—Jesus offers Himself and us to His Father. In our example, our labor and its fruits, now transformed and spiritualized into something greater than they ever were before, are joined with His sacrifice giving His Father perfect praise.

The "Amen" at the end of this prayer is one of the most important words spoken during the celebration. It is our verbal assent to everything that has happened up to this point. It is our way of saying that, yes, we do want to give our lives to God, and yes, we are willing to be transformed by Him. Indeed, between the Words of Institution and the Doxology, the transformation has already begun, for our gift has entered Jesus' heart and then entered the Father's. If transformation and renewal cannot begin there, they can never begin.

From this pinnacle, we move into the third major portion of the Eucharistic celebration, the Rite of Communion. These prayers and ceremonies prepare us to be one with God and one with His people on earth, the Body of Christ.

The first thing we do to prepare ourselves for Communion is to pray in Jesus' words—we pray the "Our Father." In praying Jesus' perfect prayer, we are saying we want to imitate Jesus' perfect attitudes toward God, toward others, and toward life, especially in any way they would affect our attitudes toward the object of our self-sacrifice—in this case, our work life. We make our verbal statement of intent to be like Jesus. This statement is required, for we would not want to be one with Jesus in Communion if we did not want to be like Him in daily life. That would be hypocrisy.

The second thing we do to prepare ourselves is to share a Sign of Peace, in effect saying that we will imitate Jesus not only in word but also in action. The Sign of Peace placed anywhere else in the celebration would have a different meaning: at the beginning of the celebration, it would be a sign of welcome; after the Penance Rite, it would be a sign of forgiveness; just before the Preparation of the Gifts, it would be a sign of solidarity among all the participants; at the end of the celebration, it would be a community commission to go forth and live the life we have pledged to live in the Eucharist. But in this place, just before receiving Communion, it has its most poignant and spiritual meaning—accepting one another and ourselves as weak and sinful yet lovable as God's children, and promising everyone we will be of some assistance to them, as they promise to be for us, in our process of transformation and renewal in the love of God.

Again, we could not truly want to be one with Jesus in Communion if we would not also want to reach out to others as He did to us with a word of encouragement and an arm that comforts and upholds. The actions of Christ are to be done now through His Body, and He underscores this point through the celebration of Eucharist. Hypocrisy reigns every time we receive Jesus but refuse His friends.

Finally, after preparing ourselves with word and action, we are ready to receive Holy Communion. We speak to the Lord in faith saying, "Say but the word and I will be healed." We address Him with these words trusting that this Communion will have a discernable effect in our lives. With these words we confess our belief that God does want us to be different because we are one with Him. These words are most effectively spoken intentionally and consciously. In unconsciousness they will not be able to open our inner selves to Him and all He can do for us.

We receive the Body and Blood of Jesus under the forms of bread and wine. We also receive what we have united with the bread and wine, that part of ourselves that He has transformed—in our example, our work life. He returns it to us because we must be responsible for ourselves—we can never give ourselves to God in the sense of giving away our integrity, dignity, or responsibility. No, this part of our lives is ours, and we will have to continue to make decisions about it. Now, however, we have the life of God in this part of us (grace) assisting us toward renewal and transformation.

Our "personal theme" has been transformed through sacrifice. Since we have given up all selfish claim on it, it can be filled with God. If it is a strength, it will no longer serve our egos but rather the Kingdom of God; if it is a weakness, it will be renewed and healed, so that it too can serve the Kingdom of God.

However, we are not the only ones who have united ourselves with the bread and wine. Others have as well, and as we receive Communion we also receive them into our hearts. This happens whether or not we want it to—it is essential to the nature of the celebration. We need to remember that receiving Communion is a free choice we make, so that if we do not want to be so closely united with others, we do not have to choose to receive Communion.

But if we freely choose to do so, we must be aware of the consequences. Receiving Communion connects us to others, and if we do not act in such a way as to express that connection, we are acting against ourselves. We are tearing our lives apart, because in one act we have decided to go in a selfless direction, but later on we decide on a selfish course. Especially because we usually do not make this choice consciously, it has a way of catching up with us. Our lives will be torn apart, all in a shambles, and we will wonder why, probably blaming all kinds of things outside ourselves, but never looking at the real culprit—our own conflicting decisions—and so never being able to do all that much to repair what has been broken.

Receiving Communion, then, is a serious act with consequences in the way we live our lives with others. It has great potential for community-making, if we choose consciously to use it. Each time we come to the Lord's Supper we freely choose to take care of each other as we take care of ourselves (the Golden Rule), and so we find another way that Eucharist humanizes us. Both on a personal and community level, we are called to be our best selves by Eucharist.

After Communion is most people's favorite time to pray for their needs, and to ask God for the wholeness, renewal and transformation that they seek. But we can see that it is the entire ceremony in which this kind of praying should be taking place. To pray for it at this time is to pray for it relatively unconsciously, expecting God to "do something" while not expecting ourselves to do much at all. When we pray for healing and renewal for the first time after receiving Communion, we are expecting the transformation without giving the sacrifice. It simply does not happen that way. By not taking our responsibility to become conscious and sacrifice ourselves to God in the first parts of the celebration, we are placing ourselves in the role of the helpless victim. We are choosing not to see how, at least in part, we got ourselves where we are, or we hold ourselves where we are. Therefore, praying for healing and renewal for the first time in our prayer after Communion is a relatively useless prayer, if we are looking for some real results.

At this point instead, if we have united ourselves with the sacrifice from the beginning, we can pray asking God to show us what He is already doing in us, the point at which He has inserted Himself in our lives to begin the process of transformation. We can pray after Communion that He reveal to us the grace of the Sacrament so that we can cooperate with it. In the case of our example, this would be the time to ask God how He is renewing our attitudes toward our labor and its fruits, how He is freeing us to be more productive, more creative, or more generous—whatever it is He has shown us to be our block toward growth in this area. As He reveals to us what He is doing—generally He will make the revelation through gentle insights in our minds and hearts, or through the subsequent happenings in our lives—we can first be grateful and then try to flow with Him.

With the last major part of the celebration completed, we conclude the Eucharist with the Dismissal Rite. Our final prayer is one of gratitude and hope, trusting that God indeed is at work in us individually and as a community. We leave with a commission from God to be responsible regarding the part of our lives we have sacrificed to Him, and to be responsible for the new life (grace) He has implanted in our "personal theme"—in our example, our work life—by acting in ways that will cooperate with that grace.

We also leave with a commission to be more the People of God than we ever were before, a commission that would be foolish if God were not now more a part of our lives than He was before. And, of course, He is more a part of us only to the degree to which we entered this celebration with a desire to sacrifice ourselves to Him. We leave with God firmly planted in a new part of our beings, giving us hope that we can be more of what He calls us to be, and more of what we want to be as we live for Him.

seven

EUCHARIST: THE FIRST HEALING SERVICE OF THE CHURCH

In Chapter 1 we briefly examined the idea that the early Christian Church saw the Eucharist as its healing service, carrying on, in a sense, the healing ministry of Jesus. As Morton Kelsey explains in his book, *Healing and Christianity* (Harper & Row, 1973), "For nearly three centuries this healing, centrally experienced, was an indispensable ingredient of Christian life" (p. 154). And much of that healing happened in connection with the Eucharistic celebration. That belief is expressed today in the Roman Rite of the Eucharist where, just before receiving Holy Communion, the celebrant and congregation pray together, "Lord, I am not worthy to receive you, but only say the word and I will be healed." Whether or not it is consciously recognized, this statement reveals a firm belief in the mind of the Church that God can and does want to heal us through the Eucharist.

The belief that God can and does heal people directly of physical, mental, and spiritual problems is part of the Apostolic tradition, as Kelsey and others have demonstrated well in both scholarly and popular works; and so this belief will not be examined here. But we will examine how Eucharist can be a way for us to connect with God's power to heal and transform, in this chapter, our own lives, and in the next chapter, the lives of others for whom we pray.

We have come to see that Eucharist is a means of self-sacrifice to God. When we open ourselves to God by emptying ourselves of selfishness, we enter a state of union and communion with Jesus, His Father and the Holy Spirit. The union God achieves with us causes transformation in our lives, for God is now filling what has hitherto been filled with ourselves. We can see, then, that if we are to seek healing through Eucharist, self-sacrifice will have to be at the center of our endeavor.

When we think of self-sacrifice, we can probably do it most easily as we consider giving to God a part of our lives of which we are proud or happy—for example, a quality of great worth, our labor and its fruits, a talent, a strength. It is easy to understand how these can be gifts precious enough to make of them a worthy sacrifice, one through which we could give to God our hearts and lives.

But at the times we will need the Eucharist to be our healing service, our strengths will not be the subject of our sacrifice—rather, we will need to sacrifice our weaknesses to God. It is not easy for us to understand, in any meaningful sense of the word, how we could be giving God our illnesses and weaknesses as a reasonable self-sacrifice, or to understand why God would even want these parts of our lives to be sacrificed to Him. Yet, if Eucharist is to bring healing into our lives, that is exactly what we will have to do.

When we speak of our weaknesses and illnesses we mean things like our darker emotions, our neediness, our painful memories, our emotional and spiritual confusion, our sinfulness, our broken relationships, our physical pain and disease, and all the parts of our personalities that we reject and therefore suppress because they threaten our egos. If a sacrifice is supposed to be a kind of gift, it is difficult for many people to understand how any of these parts of our lives could be an appropriate gift, especially to God.

Yet, when we think this way, we are not looking at ourselves from God's point of view. As Julian of Norwich, the anchoress of 14th century England, explains in her book, *Showings* (Paulist Press, 1978), while God is quite proud of and happy with our strengths, for they are the parts of our lives in which we have allowed His action and which build His Kingdom, He loves our weaknesses more, simply because they need His love more.

This concept of love is unusual in its other-centeredness. For who among us could not say that we love what is beautiful and strong in ourselves and others more than we love what is ugly and weak? But what Julian tells us is true, that our weaknesses *need* to be loved more. And it is just like God to love what, where, and when He is needed most, even though it be difficult, painful, and at times degrading to give that love. This is what Jesus did all His life. It surely is God's way.

Indeed, when we only present to God our strengths—the parts of our personalities and lives of which we are proud and happy—we are, in a sense, hiding our weaknesses from Him. There are people who live their entire lives only showing God their strong side, because they feel they need to put on a "religious mask" in order to come before God in worship. We can see the evidence of this fact in the difficulty many people have acting normally in church. As soon as they walk through the church doors, their good-natured smiles are wiped from their faces, for now it is time to be serious. The funniest comedian never could get them to laugh, because laughter is not appropriate in this setting to their way of thinking. But the truly sad aspect of this attitude is that these people often are so afraid of God they cannot find the words they need honestly to express their weaknesses and difficulties to Him. People who talk about themselves easily to friends find they talk about themselves to

God in stilted phrases, not being able accurately to describe who they are or how they feel.

God loves our weaknesses and He desires that His love will bring them into wholeness (that is, heal them). However, He wants and needs our trust to do it, and that is the great gift we give Him when we sacrifice our weaknesses to Him. For we would only reveal our weaknesses to someone we trusted. When we meet a mere acquaintance and he asks us how we are we may well answer that we are fine, even though we may have a headache and have just had an argument with someone close to us. But it is when we meet our trusted friend and she asks the same question that we pour out our hearts and tell her all about it. We reveal our weaknesses to people we trust.

Therefore, when we sacrifice our weaknesses to God telling Him all about ourselves, we are paying Him the greatest compliment. We are trusting Him not to turn His back, laugh at us, or hurt us further as we make ourselves vulnerable to Him. We are trusting His love.

When we sacrifice our weaknesses to God we are also giving Him something more—our attachments to our weaknesses. It is difficult for many people to understand that they are attached to their weaknesses, sometimes as much or more than they are attached to their strengths. But common sense, corroborated by psychological theory and observation, tells us that most every part of our personalities and lives is present to serve some purpose, because of some decision that we made, or in response to something that has happened to us in life— otherwise, it would not be there.

Therefore, all the elements of our personalities are present because we choose them to be. We find this fact easy to accept when we are speaking of our strengths. It is only when we are speaking of our weaknesses that we find it difficult to admit that in some way we choose many of our difficulties because they serve some need within us. If we did not choose at first to have them, we often choose, at least in part, to keep them. Facing this truth causes us to take responsibility for the weak areas in our lives and to give up any attitudes of self-pity, as well as to give up the role of the helpless victim, both of which are detrimental to our spiritual growth and well-being.

I once met a man whose legs were deformed by polio in his childhood. He walked only with difficulty, using canes and braces. Yet he had made in every other way quite a success of his life. He had a doctorate in sociology and was using his education in his work. He had married a beautiful wife with whom he had a tender and deep relationship, and they had two children.

In our conversation he told me that once he had had the opportunity to walk more normally. People with faith that God can heal had prayed with him, and he had taken his first steps without support in years. But then he became frightened. He knew what it meant to be handicapped. He had faced those challenges and overcome them with great strength of character. He was proud of his achievements. He was afraid of losing his identity if his legs became normal. He did not know if he could face those challenges. He had a self-concept as a successful man who had overcome his handicap, and he did not want to change that identity. He asked those people not to pray with him again, and his legs lost the strength they had gained. To this day, as far as I know, he walks only with difficulty, using canes and braces.

Our weaknesses could serve many different kinds of needs within us. An illness, for example, could be our excuse for not living more selflessly, supporting an attitude that if we do not look out for ourselves, no one else will. A weakness like fear could be our security against using gifts that would change comfortable patterns of living, supporting an attitude that we are not able to grow in creativity or productivity, an attitude we could have learned as a child and have never challenged in adulthood. A weakness like insecurity could make us seem incapable of making decisions in our lives, but always allowing us the comfortable thought that we would live life differently if we were able. All of our weaknesses, especially our illnesses, can be used to gain us the sympathy of others, something we may think we need because we see ourselves as inadequate in some basic way. And, of course, most weaknesses, especially illnesses, can give us the feeling that we have a right to self-pity, one of the reactions that is most damaging to our spiritual lives.

In explaining how we can be attached to our weaknesses, we have also demonstrated how our weaknesses and our attachments to them can be connected to our physical health and to our relationships. Of course, most of these dynamics are going on at a relatively unconscious level—that is, we may be aware of these attitudes, feelings, and reactions to some degree, but we are unaware of the great hold they have on us, of their power to control entire segments of our lives, and of the tremendous resistance we have to changing these patterns.

However, the fact that these attachments to our weaknesses are greatly unconscious makes them most suitable subjects for a sacrifice to God, in the sense that we have been exploring that topic in this book. These attachments to our weaknesses give them a power over us, so that they can even come to dominate our lives and keep us from growth. As we sacrifice them to God, we empty ourselves of their power—at first, not an entirely pleasant reality to face—and so make room for God to enter us and bring us His life in these areas in which we are experiencing a kind of death.

When we give God our attachments to our weaknesses, then, we are giving Him the great gift of freedom to make of our lives whatever He wants them to be. Therefore, essentially when we give God our weaknesses we are giving Him the same gift as when we give Him our strengths, namely, openness to growth, maturity, and His life (grace). We are also developing the gifts of faith, hope, and love, by which we come to trust God to help us and not to hurt us. This is an important part of the process of humanization, of becoming the best that human beings can be on both the psychological and spiritual planes.

Now that we understand in some way that the Eucharistic celebration can be a healing service for our physical, psychological, and spiritual weaknesses and illnesses, we need first to find our weaknesses and our attachments to them if we are going to bring them to the Eucharist for healing and renewal. We will find that many of them are unconscious, especially if they are not physical weaknesses. When they are unconscious, however, that does not mean that they are inoperative. They are expressing themselves in our lives all the time. All we need do is pay attention to our lives to discover what they are.

If we have ever tried to find our unconscious weaknesses, we know that it is not an easy thing to do, especially on our own. We need to listen to the reactions people have to us and to be sensitive to our responses to people and to situations. We can probably do this best, however, with the help of a trusted friend, whose objectivity regarding our lives will help us see our reactions clearly and discover the meanings behind them.

Or we can pray. If we do not know what our weaknesses are, this itself can be the first weakness we can sacrifice to God. In sacrificing it and praying for consciousness regarding this matter, new insights and awarenesses will begin to happen within us through Eucharistic celebration, insights that will tell us how we are sabotaging our own lives by being attached to our weaknesses.

Once we identify a particular weakness we try to name it, and to understand as well as we can how it functions within the structure of our personality. With this awareness we can bring it to Eucharist and sacrifice it to God. This weakness becomes the "personal theme" for our Eucharistic celebration which we discussed in Chapter 6.

As an example, let us say we are bringing to God a relationship with a friend broken by angry words which were fueled by pride. As we bring this broken relationship to the Opening Rite of the celebration, we begin by praising God with this situation uppermost in our minds. We thank God that this relationship has brought us to Him, making us more deeply aware of His power and His love. As we praise God in word and song, we are also allowing God to show us that He accepts us as well as the weakness we are presenting to Him—in this case, our anger and pride. He does not accept us in spite of these parts of us, as we might feel if we came to Eucharist trying to hide our weaknesses, but He accepts us with them and even because of them—the latter because they need His love to bring them into wholeness.

We continue our praise by confessing to the Lord the sin of attachment to our pride (how we resist admitting we are wrong for our part in causing and perpetuating this argument) and our anger (the attitude that the point we were trying to make was right, and she should have listened). We acknowledge how these weaknesses have prevented our growth many times over, and we also acknowledge how we have prevented our own growth in maturity and grace in this situation by not bringing it to Him sooner. As God's forgiveness is proclaimed, we believe that the celebrant's words are true, and we move into the next part of the Eucharistic celebration opened to God's life by our humility.

With this broken relationship still uppermost in our minds, we enter the first major part of the celebration, the Liturgy of the Word, in which we listen to readings from the Bible as well as the sermon or homily, expecting the Holy Spirit to speak to our hearts through the experience. In some way, He will be offering us the opportunity to have greater consciousness through the Word regarding this relationship. He may present to us a new view of the situation, helping us to see more clearly how we brought it to the broken state in which it now exists; He may ask us to forgive our friend for her mistakes in the relationship; He may suggest that we forego our right to being right, and to value relationship over being right; He may suggest we apologize for whatever we did to start or continue the argument; or He may suggest a number of other new insights that would lead to a better relationship with our friend. Whatever He communicates to us through the Word, we hear and listen, and we are grateful.

Now our consciousness regarding this situation is heightened, and we are ready to enter the next part of the celebration, the Liturgy of the Eucharist. As we prepare the bread and wine for sacrifice, prayerfully and intentionally we unite this relationship with them, making them the sacrifice of our hearts to God at this time. In the bread we place the relationship itself, especially the incident that led to its breakdown and all the angry words that were said. In the wine we place all our emotions and spiritual intuitions about the situation—our love for the person, our hurt feelings, our pride, our willfulness, our resentment and lack of forgiveness, and our attachment to having things our own way.

But most of all, we give up all attempts to tell God how to resolve this situation. This is one important way of foregoing our expectation for a return gift. For it would be a natural but selfish reaction to think that, since we have gone through all this trouble and pain to sacrifice our relationship to God, He should respond by restoring it or by restoring our dignity in it.

Rather, however, if we give something to God, it is His to do with as He sees best. If in His wisdom it is best that the relationship be restored, we can be sure He will give the grace for it; and if it is not restored, we know either that this was not His intention or—an explanation often overlooked—that we or our friend have not accepted the grace of humility and forgiveness given to us through this sacrifice. In this situation faith means trusting that, if we do our best to respond to God's grace which comes to us through this celebration, whatever happens is the best possible thing that could happen at this time in this situation. With this attitude we surrender our control and rely solely upon God for all we need.

The ceremony of worship continues with the Eucharistic Prayer, the great prayer of praise and thanksgiving of the Church. As the bread and wine are transformed into the Body and Blood of Jesus, we see and believe that the situation which we have united with the bread and wine, intending to sacrifice it to God, enters into the heart of Jesus where it, too, is transformed and renewed.

There the healing of the relationship begins immediately. However, we must remember a point we made in Chapter 3, there in reference to receiving God's Word—that when we listen our faith is not that He will say to us some particular thing (that we want to hear), but we leave Him free to say to our hearts what He thinks needs to be said. Similarly, if our faith is real—that is, truly trusting and loving—we realize that we do not know what it means to have this relationship renewed until God tells us what He is doing in it. To presume that we know what He will do far exceeds our rightful place, which is to trust that He will do something, and that it will be the right thing. While our faith is that God does specific, factual deeds which bring healing and renewal into our lives, our faith is also that we cannot tell Him what those deeds should be. When He reveals to our hearts through prayer what His intentions are, *then* we can believe with all that is in us that that specific deed will be done.

In this way, we are again sacrificing our egos and our ego-centeredness to God. As we allow God to have us and to have His way with us, we are allowing our reactions to be transformed into Christ's reactions (this is the full meaning behind the *Doxology* as it was explained in Chapter 6). This transformation is the basis of all others we hope for in our lives, even and especially if we are praying for physical healing of an illness or disease.

Completing the Liturgy of the Eucharist, we enter the third major part of the celebration, the Communion Rite. Here we prepare to receive Jesus Himself and, with Him, our "personal theme" transformed and renewed. First, we take on Jesus' attitudes toward the situation in our lives we have brought to Him for renewal—in this case, the person with whom relationship has been broken—as we pray His prayer, the Our Father. Next we promise to do the actions of Jesus, especially with this person, as we share the Sign of Peace. The Rite of Peace also has a broader application, for to the degree to which we are healed we will have more energy, and God even at this point asks us to recommit using our energy for His Church and His world. In other words, He asks us to be active and responsible members of the Body of Christ.

Then just before receiving Communion, we pray, "Lord, I am not worthy to receive you, but only say the word and I will be healed." At this most dramatic point, we are led to a statement of faith in the healing power of the Eucharist. After all, if the Eucharist is really and truly Jesus Himself, and Jesus when He lived as a human being healed anyone who came to Him in faith (even pagans), it is most reasonable that the Eucharist should bring about that same kind of healing.

Finally, we receive the Body and Blood of Christ. We believe that, even though we may not understand what God is doing or how He is doing it—in this case, transforming our broken relationship—we are receiving all we need for the renewal of this part of our lives. If we are unable to receive both the bread and wine, we believe we receive the grace for renewal of the physical aspects of this situation in the bread and the grace for renewal of the psychological and spiritual aspects in the wine. If we are able to receive the bread alone, we believe that Jesus is fully present in it with all the love we need for the healing and renewal we seek. We also at this moment accept responsibility for using the grace God is giving to us.

As we pray after Communion, we ask God to reveal what He is doing so that we can cooperate with it. It may be that He is dealing with only a part of the problem, taking the first step, as it were; it may be that He is renewing the entire situation immediately; and it may be that He is doing something completely unexpected, something for which we had not planned. We pray for the ability to cooperate with whatever He is doing in our lives, even and especially if that means that we must do something difficult like, in our example, apologize to our friend even though we still feel she was more wrong than we were.

As we close the celebration, we thank God for what He has done. We receive His blessing so that we can share it with others, and we accept His commission to take this celebration into our lives, especially into the area of our lives which we have sacrificed to Him—in this case, our broken relationship.

As we learn to celebrate Eucharist in this fashion, we will find that we can bring all kinds of difficulties to the Lord through this ceremony of worship. As we give these situations to Jesus He is able to do something about them. However—and this is important to note—we will probably find that the changes we seek will most often happen gradually, not suddenly. While all things are possible, and many have received instantaneous healing and renewal through Eucharistic celebration, that is not the ordinary case.

This is especially true when we are praying for healing of physical illnesses. Proper celebration of Eucharist demands consciousness of ourselves and our situations, as we have been discovering throughout this book. It therefore makes sense that, if we have been in the grip of an illness or other kind of weakness for a while, maybe for years, we will not easily or immediately become conscious of all the aspects of it. Rather, that process will take time, and it will take several celebrations of Eucharist to uncover and deal with all the aspects of that weakness.

There can be, however, no better way to pray for healing of

physical problems than in connection with Eucharist, especially when we are sacrificing parts of our lives to God as a way to this healing. While our self-sacrifice is never a bribe and we need to resist looking at healing as a return gift for our sacrifice, the dynamics of Eucharistic celebration make it a most effective agent for God's healing of our bodies as well as our inner selves. The Eucharist has in it great power for healing our physical illnesses, especially for three reasons: in the sacrifice we turn from our concerns to concentrate on God; we become conscious of all the ways we are attached to our illness and we give those attachments to God; and we enter into deep communion with Jesus Who is a Healer.

Regarding any type of weakness or problem, we will find that as we present our difficulties to God as we see them, celebrating the Lord's Supper in this way opens us to see our difficulties in a new light. The first change that happens in most people is that they see themselves differently, usually as more loved and lovable, and they see their responsibilities differently. From that point, God is able to lead them through a step-by-step process to more and more complete transformation. Then, as one situation is healed and transformed through a series of Eucharistic sacrifices, their eyes are opened to see the next situation on which God needs to work, and they find that they are on a pilgrimage toward wholeness and holiness.

Also, we will find that this method of celebrating Eucharist does not depend on anyone or anything but the participant alone. It therefore can be done under any circumstances. The celebration can be long or short, well performed or poorly performed, meditative or quick, simple or formal with, for example, a choir and an artistic flair. Neither does the celebrant need to understand these ideas for members of the congregation to use them, for all of these notions are a matter of attitude and internal prayer. Similarly, a celebrant can use these ideas and does not need the congregation to understand them, although the celebrant has a unique opportunity to educate the congregation as the Eucharistic sacrifice proceeds (a topic to be discussed more completely in Appendix B of this book, "Notes for Celebrants").

Most importantly, we find that every aspect of our lives can be brought to God in this way. No part of us is barred at the door of the church. On the contrary, God calls us to bring every part of ourselves, both our strengths and weaknesses, to Him for transformation, healing, and renewal. As we allow ourselves to be taken, little by little, into God's heart, we find that our lives improve on every level.

As we come to understand the true nature of Eucharist—something that can only happen as we celebrate it repeatedly yearning for consciousness—we come to understand the true nature of healing. Healing is not God denying the laws of nature because we prayed to Him; it is not our right and therefore something that we can demand from Him; and neither is it something elusive or impossible in the Modern Era. It is the simple result of emptying ourselves of selfishness, pride, and anxiety through living a life more and more formed in faith, hope, and love, so that we have room in our lives for God. When we have thus made room for Him and He resides more completely in us, He is able to bring His powerful love to bear upon our lives, and we are healed and renewed.

We also find that when we make room for Him, He is more than able to touch our lives and make them whole. He knows that when we are weak we are not able to do much more than take care of ourselves. In that state our lives lack so much of the dignity and worth they are meant to have. He heals and renews us, then, especially so that we are strong enough to build His Kingdom in the world in which we live. We find that because we have been healed and renewed by Him, the meaning of our lives unfolds, and we come to know who we are and why we were created. His life humanizes us and helps us to be His people in a unique new way. Thus we come to understand the meaning of Eucharist more deeply than ever before—it is an exchange of life that brings all the goodness of God to the world.

eight

TRANSFORMING THE WORLD THROUGH EUCHARIST

In the preceding chapters we have found that Eucharist is a dynamic and selfless mode of prayer, raising our consciousness to new heights and therefore giving us the freedom to become whole and holy people. Having found a view of Eucharist through which we can so completely identify with the other-centeredness of Christ, it is important that we keep the selfless nature of this gift intact. It is important, then, that we investigate the ways we can pray Eucharist for others, for concentrating only on praying Eucharist for ourselves may misguide us into a selfish approach toward this celebration.

Praying Eucharist for personal growth, renewal, and healing is not selfish when it is properly understood, because it is through sacrificing the entirety of our lives to God that we find the transformation we seek. As we have noted in previous chapters, the healing and renewal that come through Eucharistic sacrifice are a result of the dynamics of sacrifice itself, not a reward or a return gift God gives us when we sacrifice our lives to Him. We are healed through Eucharist precisely because we have focused our attention not on ourselves but on God, because we have not sought anything for ourselves but desired to give our hearts and lives to God.

The healing and renewal that comes through Eucharist is

not selfish for a second reason—God does not heal us for its own sake. Not that He does not want us happy, healthy, and holy— He does, and He wants us to enjoy being so. He simply does not want us to be living on this plane of well-being for ourselves alone. He also wants us to live for others.

But, when we are unconscious, weak, or sick we have little energy for caring for others and building God's spiritual Kingdom. If we were to find our identities more and more in these areas, our lives would have new dignity and new meaning. So through healing us, God is freeing us to build His Kingdom; He is making us responsible for using our strength to act in His name on earth. For whatever God heals He claims as His own, not because He is selfish, but because by claiming it He draws it into a new world of life and love, a world in which it will not be harmed or disfigured again.

However, many times people do not completely understand these notions. They can often seek personal healing and renewal as a way to "use" God's power and love for their own purposes. This motive can come out of their desperation, for example, or out of the darkness within all of us that makes us selfish. When people act this way, the entire meaning of religion is turned around, and self-sacrifice is seen as a means to receiving all we want and need from God. When we begin to seek healing for its own sake, we are falling into a spiritual self-centeredness, a spiritually dangerous position which we will need to correct and counterbalance.

It is important, then, as we study the Eucharist to see how we can pray this great prayer for others as well as for ourselves. As we learn to give Eucharist as a gift to others we will be purifying our spirituality from selfishness by learning to give a valuable gift. For after understanding how much we need Eucharist for our personal growth and well-being, it is a great gift to pray it not for ourselves but for another.

And on a broader note, Eucharistic sacrifice is the most

powerful means we have to participate through prayer in God's creation and redemption of the world. Christ has commissioned us to bring Him to all the world through our love, both in action and in prayer. We could find no greater and more effective means to bring Jesus to the world through prayer than joining in His continuous self-sacrifice to His Father through Eucharist.

We have seen how, as we sacrifice ourselves to God in Eucharist, we are transformed—that is, recreated, redeemed, and humanized. Through Eucharist more and more of our lives is brought into relationship with God. When others become the object of our sacrifice—when we sacrifice so that they receive the life that transforms and recreates—they, too, can be humanized; they, too, can receive the grace of renewal and healing. We then become people who help bring the world into life, the life of self-sacrifice that is Eucharist. In other words, sacrificing Eucharist for others will help us to appreciate the fact that we are connected with others by spiritual bonds—that we are, in other words, members of the Body of Christ on earth.

One of the ways, then, that we can give Eucharist as a gift is to pray it for another person. When we want to pray for someone who is sick or otherwise in need, when we want to bless another, when we desire a spiritual reconciliation with someone with whom we have a troubled relationship, we can pray Eucharist for that person or persons with great effectiveness in their lives and, secondarily but no less importantly, in our own. Often we have a desire to pray for others but we do not have a way to do it. We pray for a while and become distracted, or even bored. Then we feel guilty because we are not praying as we promised or as we desire. Eucharist can be a focused prayer through which we find we can give the gift of love to others.

To pray in this way what we need to do is to keep the other person constantly in mind throughout the Eucharistic celebration. The other becomes, as it were, our "personal theme" for the Eucharist.

This is not an off-handed kind of intention whereby at the beginning of the celebration we simply say, "I offer this Eucharist for so-and-so," and proceed to forget about that person throughout the rest of the ceremony of worship. Rather, it is an intense kind of giving of self as we keep the other person's intentions or needs in mind as completely and with as much investment as if they were our own. Just as we have described sacrificing a part of our lives through Eucharist in Chapter 6 and sacrificing a weakness in Chapter 7, so we proceed in consciousness and love for another as we present his or her needs to God, asking God to give to this person the gifts of consciousness and spiritual life He would have given to us through this prayer if we had prayed it for ourselves.

For example, we pray that the vulnerability to grace we would receive through praising Him in the Opening Rite He would instead give to the other person. We ask that the understanding of God and life we would have received through His Word He would give to that person.

We can also be praying throughout the beginning of the celebration that God will make us more conscious of the real needs of this person, and that He will make us more compassionate for this person through our praise and receiving His Word. Indeed, this kind of praying can help us to "walk a mile in another person's moccasins," as the old Indian metaphor phrases it, because we are taking on this person's pain or need. Through it we can come to see the other person's life more from his or her own point of view, and thus to pray with that same investment with which we pray when we sacrifice our own lives to God.

As the gifts of bread and wine are prepared, then, it is not our own life that we sacrifice with these offerings, but the life of the other person. We prayerfully and intentionally unite the physical aspects of his or her need with the bread, the psychological and spiritual aspects with the wine. And when we join in the Eucharistic Prayer, the great prayer of thanksgiving of the Church, we do so bringing this person into the sacrifice, lovingly asking Jesus to accept him or her into His heart for renewal, healing and transformation.

Of course, it is important that we pray with as much consciousness as possible regarding any self-righteous feelings we may have. To have them is simply a temptation; to pray with them as a motive is destructive of ourselves and the person for whom we pray. As we become aware of any feelings that are encouraging us to pray for this person because we do not like the person the way he or she is, or because we want to see the person's life change to please ourselves (this kind of attitude could be present in subtle forms such as, "She needs so much help" or "The poor thing's life is such a mess, he needs prayer"), we simply offer these feelings to God as our own sacrifice of consciousness. We seek forgiveness for them, asking that we pray for the other only from a motive of love—that is, caring for the other for his or her own sake, wanting to see the best happen in that person's life.

Similarly, if there is any selfishness in our prayer—that is, if we are praying for this person because if God did thus-and-so in his or her life it would make our own lives easier—we also confess these intentions to God begging forgiveness, and asking that they be replaced with His own selfless love for the person as our motivation for prayer. We can see that one of the personal effects of praying for others in this fashion is that we will be confronted with our own negative attitudes and thus given the opportunity to let go of them. This can be a painful process of self-awareness, but it is one that will make our relationship with the other person much stronger and holier.

As we prepare for Communion through the Our Father and the Rite of Peace, we ask that the openness to God's grace that we would receive through these prayers be given to the other person. As we receive Communion, we ask that the transformation and healing we would receive through this Sacrament be given to the other person. As we pray after Communion, we ask that the other person be able to cooperate with the grace he or she is receiving, and to accept the support, insight, and hope that God is giving.

Similarly to the previous parts of the Eucharistic celebration, during the Communion Rite we are also praying that we can be as selfless as possible in our prayer for the other. We ask that God open our hearts to appreciate the depth of the other's need—not objectively, as if we are separate from the other (and therefore creating a probability of judging the other), but from within the other person's own frame of reference. We look at the other's life from his or her point of view, from within his or her mind. To put it in a word, we pray compassionately (not with pity, which carries a note of condescension). Compassion, of course, humanizes us, and we are healed as our hearts are expanded to love more deeply.

To pray in this way is an intense experience of love and relationship. It is a true gift of something precious, for we are giving the love of Jesus to another through our own love. If we were to give our own love alone, our gift would be generous but only as powerful to help the person as we are on our own and unassisted by God. If we were to attempt to give Jesus' love alone, our gift would be impersonal and, in that sense, no gift at all. But when we allow Jesus to use our own human hearts as a channel for His love, not only is our gift made precious and powerful because of our personal investment in it, but we too are able to receive a gift.

If we are praying Eucharist for people who are sick or otherwise in need, we can pray for their well-being throughout the celebration, sacrificing their particular problems to God, and letting go of any egotistical notions we have about how God should help them, as well as any selfish motives that they be freed from their illness or weakness to make our lives easier. If we are praying for a blessing for people we love, we can let go through sacrifice of any selfish attachment to them, asking God to bless them and encourage them to be their best selves—even and especially if we seem to have strong desires for their lives contrary to their own, as often happens, for example, in parents as they pray for their children; and even and especially if their growth in what God desires for their lives means that we will not receive from them what we want to receive in relationship.

If we are praying for people with whom we are not in good relationship, the Eucharist can be a powerful prayer of forgiveness. We can pray Eucharist for such people asking God to bless them through the sacrifice, and to bless them whether or not they change to our liking. For when we are angry with people and need to forgive them, what we are saying is that we want them to change. Eucharist becomes a means of putting aside our conditions for accepting them and simply receiving them into our hearts, appreciating them the way they are. Through Eucharist we can pray that God bless them and make them happy in the way that would please them the most, whether or not they ever make *us* happy. In this selfless prayer, we sacrifice our egos and become humanized, and we allow the people for whom we pray the freedom they need to grow as their own lives, and not our needs, direct them.

Another way of describing what this kind of celebration does to us is to say that it breaks the *participation mystique* we have with others, allowing them to be themselves in all their uniqueness. When we begin to identify with another through the *participation mystique*, we destroy a part of that person's individuality as well as a part of our own. Praying Eucharist in this way can begin to free us and others to be more whole people, taking responsibility for our own individuality, and not using this over-identification with another as an excuse for not growing ourselves.

A second way we can pray the Sacrament of the Lord's

Supper for other people can happen when we celebrate Eucharist as a part of a special event—for example, a wedding, a baptism, a birthday, or an anniversary. Many of us participate in such celebrations and enjoy having Eucharist be a part of them, but we are not conscious of the powerful means it could be to dedicate to God the person or persons we are celebrating. Instead of sharing Eucharist relatively unconsciously—that is, thinking of it as a way "to bring God into the occasion"—we can celebrate it with the consciousness which we have been discovering in this book as a way to bring other people's lives to the Lord for renewal and transformation.

We can celebrate Eucharist at a special event as a gift to the people who are being honored, in a similar manner to the way we described praying Eucharist for those in need, but this time in thanksgiving for their lives, and asking God to bless them with greater consciousness and grace. We remain conscious of those being honored all through the celebration, asking God through each part of it to give to them whatever blessing or grace would come to us if we were celebrating Eucharist sacrificing our own lives to Him. We can also be praying to love those people more, and so to be humanized—to pray for the expansion of our own hearts that comes with spiritual love and compassion.

A third time that we can celebrate Eucharist in such a way as to improve the world in which we live is at the beginning of a project we are undertaking. As many people begin a new venture they come to God and ask for His blessing, and many do this by celebrating Eucharist. But simply to ask God to bless what we do leaves us relatively unconscious regarding that venture. We may, in a sense, be trying to use God when we ask Him to bless a project but do not open ourselves to hear whether He has any guidance for it or even whether He approves of it at all.

If, however, we were to sacrifice that project consciously to

God, we would be letting go of our selfish claims on it, making it possible for that venture to be so filled with Him that it could be a vehicle He could use for His purposes. From this point of view we can see the value, whether or not it has been our custom in the past to seek God's blessing for a project, of sacrificing our endeavor to Him so that it can be a selfless venture, helping to bring His light into the world.

As we celebrate Eucharist first praising God for the opportunity that this project is creating for us; then receiving through His Word any insights, encouragement, correction, etc., He may want to give us; and finally offering Him the physical aspects of the project through the bread and the psychological and spiritual aspects through the wine, we are bringing yet another piece of creation back to its Creator.

We celebrate the Lord's Supper with this project as our "personal theme" and we come to consciousness regarding it. We receive Communion, then, trusting that God is giving us what we need to do the project well and to do it selflessly, that is, for Him and for His glory. After Communion we ask Him how we can best cooperate with the life He is giving us, and we ask Him to help us keep our intentions for this venture pure and holy. In this way, even the smallest of projects becomes another part of the Kingdom of God in this world, and our love of God allows it to be so.

A fourth way we are able to transform our world through Eucharistic celebration can happen when we hear of events near or far that are of public concern—for example, a disaster, a national or international conflict, or a public controversy. We can sacrifice this situation to the Lord as a way of interceding for it. So often we honestly want God to be more present in these kinds of situations, but we do not know how to pray for them. We try to hold them in our minds for a while and believe that God is giving the life that is necessary to confront the destructive elements of the situation, but soon we lose interest or become distracted. Bringing these concerns to Eucharist can be an effective way to focus our prayer for them, and to bring life to them.

So often when we pray for such concerns, we pray in a relatively unconscious manner, asking for a "blessing" in the situation—as in the prayer, "God, please bless the firemen on strike, and let the strike be over soon," or "Lord, please bring peace to that troubled part of the world, and help those waging the war to come to the bargaining table to address their grievances." While the sentiment behind these prayers is commendable, it is unfortunately often not much more than that, for these prayers are a type of "religious wishing," not praying in faith. In other words, this is another example of wanting transformation without first making the sacrifice. It simply does not happen that way.

Bringing these concerns to a celebration of the Lord's Supper would be a much more powerful way to pray for them, if we celebrate that Eucharist in the way we have been describing in this book—that is, concentrating on the concern through each part of the celebration, seeing how it relates to each part of the celebration, and finally sacrificing the physical aspects of it to God in the bread and the interior aspects of it in the wine, with all the fervor we would have if we were sacrificing an important part of our own lives to God.

With concerns like disasters, we selflessly present the needs of others to God as carefully as if they were our own. Our self-sacrifice is one of love for others, and so our hearts are expanded and humanized.

With concerns like international conflicts and public controversies, we let go of our egocentrism by letting go of our opinions and attitudes regarding the situation, for they can prevent us from seeing it from God's point of view and therefore praying more powerfully. In so doing we are simultaneously relinquishing our need to be right. We sacrifice all the elements of the situation to God, asking that all people, including ourselves, be enlightened to see in which ways they are right and in which ways they are wrong, and to have the gracefulness to seek forgiveness and to change. We also can pray for these situations by sacrificing the needs of the people who are involved in and possibly hurt by the situation.

A fifth opportunity we have to pray for others through Eucharistic celebration and thus add something to the world in which we live is on the occasions of national holidays or days on which we are celebrating the Church. If we celebrate Eucharist as a part of these occasions we can pray for the State and/or the Church, reconsecrating these bodies to God by sacrificing them and our part in them to Him.

Regarding national holidays, again we know that many people make Eucharist a part of their celebration of them. This desire to make God a part of their civic life could be used in a powerful way to allow His spiritual authority to affect the State through prayer. Instead of simply thanking God for our country, for example, we could be sacrificing it to Him, seeking His wisdom and justice to guide national policy, and offering as our self-sacrifice our attitudes and opinions regarding the nation, asking Him to form in us His ideas on these matters.

Regarding celebrations of the Church, we can again grow in consciousness of our attitudes, ideas, and feelings about the People of God as we celebrate Eucharist, and we can seek His guidance and spiritual gifts to fill us. Our self-sacrifice is our life of service in and through the Church, as well as our opinions and prejudices about it, and we can ask God to take those parts of our lives and do with them whatever He wants. This sacrifice of self gives us the privilege of offering the Church to God so that He can continue to renew it. In this way we can also pray for unity among churches as we sacrifice our own as well as others' self-righteous attitudes, grudges, hostilities, and resentments, then asking God to help us devote ourselves to the higher goals of peace and love in the Body of Christ.

We have too little understanding and appreciation of the

power of Eucharist to transform our world. The power is surely present whenever we celebrate Eucharist, because Jesus is always present as He promised, and His desire is that the world be transformed.

That transformation will happen only as we bring the world to Christ, for "when everything is subjected to him, then the Son himself will be subject in his turn to the One who subjected all things to him, so that God may be all in all" (1 Cor 15:28). But channeling that power is our task. We can only do it as we sacrifice our egotistical opinions and ideas as well as our selfish attitudes and feelings to God, so that we are open to His way of responding to the world. We become able to transform the world through our Eucharistic sacrifice by allowing God to humanize our hearts and minds. In other words, by expanding our consciousness to love all creation, even as He loves all creation, we help bring the world to the Father in Christ.

God is capable of doing this great deed in and through us. However, He first needs our response to the request He makes of all of us—that we be stretched and our hearts expanded, until we become like Him.

nine

THE POWER OF EUCHARISTIC LOVE

The celebration of Eucharist brings to earth the power of the Resurrected Jesus. He is Master of the universe, Savior of mankind, and Healer of our physical and inner selves. But most of all, He loves. He cares deeply about everything and everyone, each individually, as if that person or thing were the only creature in the world. The Eucharist is Jesus in His resurrected state, just as really as He was present on earth after His resurrection centuries ago. The Eucharistic celebration allows Him to be present everywhere His Church is, and it allows Him to reveal His love in many places and circumstances. All over the globe, Jesus is present among His people physically and spiritually through the Eucharistic sacrifice.

No wonder, then, that the custom of saving some of the Eucharistic bread (and, at times, the wine) began early in the history of the Church and is carried on by many Christian Churches today. Not only does this custom allow the Eucharist to be brought to the sick who cannot participate in the full celebration so that they, too, might benefit from its renewing and healing power, but this custom also allows us all to come before the Eucharist and pray, continuing to seek and find the life it brings to the world.

In the Roman Catholic Church, the custom of reserving the Sacrament has allowed development over the years of various customs that honor the presence of Jesus in the Eucharist both through private prayer and public services. The spirituality that underlies one of these services, called Benediction (derived from the Latin words *bene* and *dicere* which literally mean "to speak well," or, in other words, to praise or bless), has much to teach us about the nature of the Eucharist and how we can find its healing and transforming power today.

In this ceremony of praise and worship, the Eucharistic bread, called the Host (from the Latin word *hostia*, which means "sacrifice"), is placed in a sacred vessel called a Monstrance (from the Latin word *monstrare*, which means "to show" and from which English words like *demonstrate* find their origin). The Monstrance is made of metal and is usually designed to represent a sunburst, with the Host displayed in a glass container in the place of the sun. The sunburst representation is on a stand between one and two feet high, which allows the Host to be seen by everyone in the Church when the Monstrance is placed on the altar. With the Eucharist visible in their midst, the congregation sings and praises God for the wonder of His love.

The construction of the Monstrance gives us a clue to what is happening in this ceremony of worship and praise. It tells us of a deep spiritual truth: Jesus in the Eucharist is the source of tremendous spiritual energy which radiates from His presence to all who are there in faith to receive. As the people praise and worship God, forgetting about themselves and becoming lost in His wonder and beauty, just as they are called to do in the Eucharistic celebration, they become open to that energy and it fills them. Just in the same way that we cannot walk in the sunlight without being warmed by its rays, so we cannot be in the presence of the Eucharist without being filled with Jesus' love, to the degree we are open to it through faith.

Jesus is always available to fill us with life in the Eucharist reserved in the tabernacle. His energy is as limitless as His love.

As we learn to come before Him and receive, we find that here is a great spiritual power to help us with our needs and concerns.

One of the places in which people have found this spirituality to be helpful is in the counseling and healing center which is one of my apostolates to administrate. As people come to the center for help, and as our counselors and prayer therapists prepare to minister to others, one of the first things we ask all of them to do is to pray before the Eucharist in our chapel for at least a half hour, so that they can praise God and receive His love into the center of their beings. We ask them to imagine what is spiritually true (we find that imagining it helps people to be open to it happening discernibly within them): that Jesus in the Eucharist is a source of divine light, and all they need do is relax and receive His light into themselves.

This kind of prayer is a form of self-sacrifice, carrying on the prayer of the Eucharistic celebration. Simply coming before the Eucharist in this way is a sacrifice of time which people could spend in ways that would seem to many to be more useful. As they pray before the Eucharist they are offering their lives to Jesus for Him to affect them in whatever way He wishes. They are praising Him by concentrating on Him—on His light and His love. As they lose themselves in Him they are sacrificing their egos, and they receive the fruits of self-sacrifice.

The results of this simple prayer time are amazing. First, people enter their counseling sessions in a much more peaceful and centered state. Sometimes they already have insight into their problem. Always their sessions with their counselors are more productive, proceeding faster and easier than those times at which they did not follow this practice. And when it comes time for prayer for transformation and healing, it happens with greater freedom, wisdom, insight, and results.

I have personally experienced the healing and transforming power of prayer before the Eucharist at times in which I have been in distress. Just recently I was having an argument with a friend. When we seemed to be in a deadlock we each took time out for prayer, and I went to pray before the Eucharist. In less than ten minutes of receiving the Lord's healing light I was laughing at myself and the situation, and I was able to go back and retreat from my intellectual position so that I could love with my heart. From that point on my friend and I found ourselves able to communicate and to sort out our differences.

Another example of the power of this kind of prayer comes from a Day of Renewal I was asked to give to a group of people who confused and bewildered me. Their problems with each other and with various unusual spiritualities distressed me, and I wondered if I could minister to them at all. I had lost most of my confidence, not only because of the difficult situation they presented, but also because I was personally anxious over some matters and had not slept well the night before.

I entered the auditorium a little over an hour before the program was to begin. Since there was nothing I could do to set up for the program, I had time to seek out the Eucharist and to pray as I described above, imagining spiritual energy emanating from the Eucharist filling me with God's light. By the end of the hour I was not only relaxed and my spirits lifted, but I also had direction for my presentations and love for the people to whom I was to give them.

One of the most important aspects of this kind of prayer is that we say little. It is a type of "centering prayer," a time to become more deeply in touch with our own emotions and reactions, seeing and feeling them for what they are, and to be in touch with God's reactions to us. As we simply present our-selves to Jesus and allow His light to shine in and through us, He reveals the truth about our situations. He may show us that the basis for our problem is in negative attitudes of which we have to this point been unconscious. He may, on the other hand, want to comfort us because of some difficulty or trauma we have endured and pretended did not hurt us. Whatever He does, the point is that we allow Him to do it, and we give Him that permission by not filling our time with verbalizing our needs. We simply come to Him in faith that His light will reveal the problem and His love will create the way to a solution.

We must never forget that when we pray before the Eucharist we are in the presence of God Himself. When we come into prayer before God, so many of us are used to speaking more than to receiving. But God is One to Whom we can make ourselves vulnerable in quiet, and as we imagine what is spiritually true—that His love and light are streaming forth into our entire beings—we find we are known and accepted. To gaze upon the Eucharist in this way with spiritually enlightened eyes is a preparation for what heaven will be. There our defenses will no longer be necessary, and we will be able to be filled completely with Him, merging our hearts with His, our minds and wills with His, our entire beings with His.

It is important, then, that we not take this gift for granted. To pray before the Eucharist whenever we can, and to acknowledge the fact that we need this power in our lives more than we have previously admitted, is that attitude of humility that allows God to be for us. So often we want God to act in our lives, but we do not stay in His presence long enough for Him to work. Prayer before the Eucharist in stillness will fill us with those spiritual gifts we need in order to accomplish the Lord's mission for our lives.

It is Jesus' self-sacrificing love that makes being still before the Eucharist so powerful in our personal prayer. To be in the presence of that selfless love energizes us, for we also are made to live selflessly. That selfless love is the center of the universe, and when we are bathed in that love we are in relationship to the center and the origin of all creatures. His is a love that gives life, a love that makes whole everything it touches. His is a love that humanizes us, making us the best we can be. His is the love we have been seeking all our lives, and it completes us as we allow it into our deepest selves.

Simply being in the presence of Jesus' selfless love makes

us accountable regarding the quality of our own love. He challenges us to allow our hearts to be stretched and expanded, so that we will be living more and more in His image. Similarly, Jesus challenges all we have learned from the world in which we live, especially those ideas that encourage us to live for ourselves. He tells us, just by His presence, that the best way to live and the happiest way to live is for others. This kind of life certainly can be demanding as His life was, but it will also yield all that His life did. Jesus calls us to consciousness as He gives us what we need, asking us to share the gift with others—to give the gift we have received (cf. Mt 10:8). As He has filled with love the emptiness within us, He wants us to fill the emptiness in others with the same gift.

The Sacrament of the Eucharist, then, continues the power of the celebration of the Lord's Supper. In the Eucharistic celebration Jesus continues the sacrifice He made on the cross, giving Himself totally to His Father. But now through this celebration He draws all His people into the same selfless act, uniting human beings with His Father again. In the Eucharistic celebration Jesus helps us to sacrifice our lives to our Father through self-awareness and foregoing any selfish claims on our lives.

As we pray before the Sacrament of the Eucharist, we are again called to self-knowledge and awareness of the egotistic claims we make on our own and others' lives. We are again challenged to forego that which holds us down, and to receive that which lifts us up. Immediately, as with the Eucharistic celebration, we are aware, however, that we are responsible for that which we have received. For this is the movement of true spirituality, a movement outward, a movement toward God and others.

So again we find essential to a complete understanding of Eucharist the teaching that the Church is the Body of Christ on earth. Eucharistic worship is incomplete if it does not flow into

Christian community in some concrete way. Through the Eucharist Jesus continues to transform our weak personalities into images of Himself, not only for our own edification but also for the edification of the community.

This sunburst of selfless love begins in the celebration of the Lord's Supper and continues throughout time. Jesus continues His love in this physical and real way because He knows how much we need Him, He knows we always need to grow in consciousness, and He is so selfless He wants to be available to us at all times. The Sacrament of the Eucharist opens for us a window to the spiritual world, so that we can continue our search for God and for the wholeness and holiness He gives when we sacrifice ourselves to Him.

ten

RESOLVING DIFFICULTIES WITH EUCHARISTIC CELEBRATION

There are many people both within and outside of Churches that celebrate Eucharist who have difficulties with the beliefs and practices that surround the Lord's Supper. In a book that so strongly presents Eucharistic faith as central to spirituality, it is important to investigate some of these difficulties and their validity. Also, as we examine the ideas and approaches of this book in relationship to these difficulties, they may help some people through them, or at least may help them to consider some new attitudes toward them.

One of these difficulties is expressed in varying degrees by people who now celebrate Eucharist: they are put off by the community interaction that has become a part of Eucharistic celebration in recent years. (In the Roman Catholic Church, these practices were initiated in the mid-1960's with the liturgical reforms which resulted from the teachings of the Second Vatican Council.) These people object to being asked, for example, to sing aloud, to pray aloud, and especially to greet the people around them in the Sign of Peace.

Many of these people say that these activities distract them from worshiping God. They are used to other customs, older practices of keeping silence in church, and a view of worship that is private and interior. When now they are asked to change these principles, they become confused and sometimes even angry. What they are asked to do now does not seem to them to be worship.

Throughout this book we have been investigating a particular psychological and spiritual view of Eucharist that has something to say to those who do not find community participation an important part of worship. Since for many people the focus of their problems with community participation is the Sign of Peace, let us review what we discovered in Chapter 6 regarding the Communion Rite, of which the Sign of Peace is a part, to see how it applies to this difficulty.

The Communion Rite is the last major part of the Eucharistic celebration. The primary object of the Communion Rite is to call us to imitate Christ in various ways, so that we will be ready to receive Him in Communion. For Communion is that act by which we become one with Jesus, and we need to prepare ourselves for it by choosing to live in the way He lives.

We begin the Communion Rite with the Our Father, in which we repeat the words of Christ, asking that the attitudes they convey become our own attitudes: revering the Father, submitting to His authority, being open to receive His gifts, acknowledging and receiving His forgiveness for our mistakes and sins, seeking His help to forgive others, seeking His protection from evil, and giving Him praise for all His work. In other words, this prayer calls forth from us a sacrifice of our egocentrism to the Father, entirely changing our reasons to live from selfish ones to selfless ones.

In the Rite of Peace we follow through on what we have just said in the Our Father. Words without actions to back them up are worse than useless. If we say the words of the Our Father without intending to act on them, we are merely repeating Jesus' words in a relatively unconscious way, not hearing what they expect of us, not allowing ourselves to be converted by them. Our prayer then becomes a lie of sorts, for it would be *mere* words, that is, our words would not be referring to any reality in our lives.

The Rite of Peace gives us the opportunity immediately after saying the words of Christ to allow them to create their own reality in us. In the Rite of Peace we are doing the actions of Christ—in other words, we are following through on the Our Father. In this rite we extend ourselves through word and gesture to the people around us and share with them the well-being Jesus has given to us. We are imitating the actions of Christ Who was always a peacemaker, a reconciler, and Who extended His love freely to all. The more consciously we imitate the actions of Christ, the more our hearts are expanded and humanized into the image of Christ.

In receiving Holy Communion, we complete our progression toward union with Jesus. Our first step was in word, our second in action, and our final step in being. By receiving Communion we are saying that there is no part of our lives that we do not want to be one with Christ, that there is nothing that He thinks, feels, or does that we would not want to imitate. As with the Our Father and the Rite of Peace, however, we can receive Communion consciously or unconsciously—in other words, aware to varying degrees of what we are doing and its consequences. The act of receiving Communion is a freely chosen one, with consequences that flow from it. It is a commitment to thinking, feeling, and behaving in a particular way, in the way of Jesus.

As we can see, each part of the Communion Rite builds on the one before it, just as the entire Communion Rite builds on (and would not make sense without) all the parts of the Eucharistic celebration before it. The oneness the Communion Rite aims at effecting between us and God depends on our sacrificing our selfishness in the Liturgy of Eucharist; our ability to sacrifice ourselves to God without seeking a return gift in the Liturgy of the Eucharist builds on the raising of our consciousness of the quality of our lives in the Liturgy of the Word; our ability to receive God's Word into our hearts depends upon the personal vulnerability created through praise and forgiveness in the Opening Rite. It then makes sense to say that, to the degree to which we are unconscious of, in disagreement with, or distracted during any part of the Eucharistic celebration, the culmination of that celebration—receiving Communion—will be diminished in its effect, both for ourselves and for the world in which we live. We will be less open to God's grace personally as well as to God living through us in the world.

Therefore, it is obvious that the Rite of Peace is placed quite strategically within the Communion Rite. It is calling us to accountability for imitating Christ *before* we become one with Christ. It is calling us to consciousness regarding the social nature of what we are about to do. If we choose to "go through the motions" in the Rite of Peace, we are in effect telling God we want Him to "go through the motions" when we receive Communion. If we fold our arms and refuse to participate in the Rite of Peace, we are folding our arms to God as well, for "in so far as you neglected to do this to one of the least of these, you neglected to do it to me" (Mt 25:46). On the other hand, if we sacrifice our selfishness and participate in the Sign of Peace, we invite the fruits of Jesus' self-sacrifice on the Cross into our own hearts. In other words, our Sign of Peace must be heartfelt and sincere if we are to have a heartfelt and sincere relationship with God.

Holy Communion itself is also a social Sacrament and not only a private, personal devotion. For in it we receive Jesus Who has come to dwell in the bread and wine, which has also become a symbol of our own lives. However, we have not been the only people who have united ourselves with the bread and wine—everyone else there has, too. Therefore, whenever we receive

Communion we not only receive Jesus, and we not only receive back the part of ourselves we sacrificed with Him to the Father now healed and transformed, but we also enter more deeply into union with everyone else who is participating in Eucharist. Indeed, we are in union with everyone who has ever at any time or place participated in the Eucharistic sacrifice.

Communion, of its nature, connects us to the other members of the Body of Christ. This is one reason that the Communion bread is called the Body of Christ and the Church as well is called the Body of Christ. One creates the other; they create each other.

But many people receive Communion while choosing to ignore this element of what they are doing. Ignoring it, however, makes it no less true. By receiving Communion we freely choose to be one with all of Christ, Himself and His Body—for Jesus simply will not and, indeed, cannot separate Himself from His Body. If we do not want to be one with Jesus *and* with His Body, we cannot sincerely receive Communion. But when we refuse to participate in the Rite of Peace or we participate in it half-heartedly, and then we do make the statement that we want to be one with the Body of Christ by receiving Communion, we are simply not being honest.

If, however, we *are* honest with ourselves and with the Lord, we will accept the "spiritual-social" nature of the Eucharistic celebration—that is, we will accept the fact that Jesus wants to unite people with Himself and with each other through Eucharist. If the Rite of Peace raises in us emotions of anger and fear toward others which cause us to withdraw from them, then it is doing us a favor! For it is pointing out to us the unwholeness within us so that we can present it to Jesus for healing. It is graphically demonstrating to us that we need to celebrate Eucharist with open hands, and to give up the selfishness from which most anger and negative feelings spring.

Addressing our problems with individual people or with

people in general raises our consciousness and gives us the opportunity to choose holiness. As we admit our difficulties with people we are being more honest—we are describing our lives as they are and not trying to hide the truth, or to hide from it. Admitting these difficulties also reveals that our problem is not with the ceremony of the Eucharist or with the Rite of Peace. It is with people. From this point of honesty we can begin to grow and change.

For the solution to our problem with people is to forgive them, and when we do that we are accepting them and loving them as they are, withdrawing from them our need for them to change. When we see a need for others to change, excluding ourselves from this requirement, we call what we are doing "projection." We project onto others when we see in them the fault we have but will not consciously admit, and we become angry with them for having the fault we have. They may have that fault, too, but that is not the point; for unless we admit that we have the fault we continue to be angry with others and not to seek the healing *we* need.

But when we withdraw our projections and forgive others, we allow ourselves to grow, and we allow them to grow as well. Growth is also possible when we choose to accept others who are different from ourselves in aptitude, holiness, physical size or strength, emotional constitution, education, family, background, race, sex, color, or creed. Whenever we can withdraw barriers to unity in Christ among people, we are aiding psychological wholeness and spiritual growth in ourselves and others, the total humanization of mankind.

Therefore, the Rite of Peace is both a gift to us and a work to accomplish in grace and honesty. We need not be surprised when it or any other part of the Eucharistic celebration brings up feelings in us totally opposite to love and unity. These feelings are sometimes the result of pain we feel from the actions of other people in our lives and from our own decisions, and at other times they come from the ways we cling to attitudes and beliefs that encourage our selfishness. Knowing about this pain is a gift, for only when these feelings are conscious can we choose to confront them, to change any attitudes which may cause them, and to let God heal them. Only when we know about them can we bring them to Jesus in Eucharistic celebration for healing and transformation.

When we experience these feelings, then, we are aware that they are common reactions in many people. That knowledge, however, is no reason to remain controlled by them, especially when we see what they do to the integrity of our Eucharistic celebration. When they come forth in situations like the Rite of Peace, they do so precisely so that we can be freed from them through Eucharistic self-sacrifice. As we choose to do what we sometimes do not feel like doing—in this case, to reach out and express care for others just because they are there, as Jesus would—God is able to transform our small hearts, expanding them to be a little more like His. This process of being humanized will bring wholeness and holiness into our lives as well as into the lives of the people around us.

Another difficulty that some people have with Eucharistic celebration is, to put it simply, they find it boring. Some of these people "attend" Eucharist (they do not participate much) merely out of a sense of obligation—in other words, they think it is the right thing to do although it seems lifeless, or they know it is what others expect of them and they do it, even though it means little to them. Others say that it is not "satisfying worship," and that they can worship God better alone or in nature. It is impossible for most of us to escape these feelings to one degree or another unless we have come to understand the compelling and personal nature of Eucharistic self-sacrifice, at least at some level of consciousness.

It is also worthy to note that while younger people are usually freer in verbalizing these kinds of feelings, older people often experience them no less. And while some people are freer to act upon these feelings and therefore they cease celebrating Eucharist, other people tend to repress the feelings, to continue "attending" Eucharist, and to allow these now unconscious feelings to limit their participation in effective and heartfelt worship.

The result in any case is boredom, and it is a common problem many people have with Eucharistic celebration. Let us, then, investigate boredom as people experience it in Eucharist.

When we find that anything is boring, one of the things we are saying is that we cannot relate to it, that we have not found a way to become involved in it. There is nothing more boring than, for example, watching a sports event unless we can somehow find a way to identify with a team or person, or to become excited over the skill of the athletes—in other words, to connect ourselves personally with the event. Similarly, we need to find some way to identify with, to become involved with the Eucharistic celebration in order to find it exciting and interesting.

Throughout this book we have come to understand more deeply the psychological and spiritual dynamics of the Lord's Supper, and as we have done so we have seen that the celebration, by its nature, calls for tremendous personal involvement. It is indeed when we are not involved in it that we vitiate its meaning and value. If the celebration calls forth our involvement naturally, the reason that some people are not involved in it and rather are bored must be either that they do not understand the dynamics of the celebration or that they resist becoming involved in it.

When people are bored with Eucharist, they will often verbalize their feelings by saying that they do not see the value in Eucharist, or that they can worship God better in some other way, or that they can see no need to worship God at all. In saying such things, they often are projecting outside of themselves one of several difficulties which center more in their own attitudes than in God or in Eucharistic celebration.

They could, for example, be resisting the notion which is at the heart of self-sacrifice—that is, giving up control of their lives. Many people in our culture have developed strong attitudes of self-sufficiency and independence, and when they come face-to-face with Jesus and His total lack of control over His life, they cannot or will not see the transcendence of His way, because they and their way of life are too threatened by it.

Another difficulty they could be having is that Eucharist calls forth from us an involvement so deep it seems at times too much to ask. Eucharistic self-sacrifice expects a great maturity from us, and it challenges us to develop an even greater maturity. People who are bored or unsatisfied with their Eucharistic celebration may then, in reality, not understand the compelling nature of this celebration, or they may not want to accept the tremendous challenge to maturity it offers.

Yet another difficulty they could be having is resisting the call to consciousness. Many people are highly invested in remaining unconscious, for becoming conscious would necessitate that they give up comfortable habits of thought or behavior, psychological games by which they control other people, or attitudes which allow themselves privileges without which they have decided they cannot live.

A fourth difficulty they could be having is resisting the call to selflessness. They do not want to give up their claims for a return gift in exchange for the gift of their life to God. In a culture that is based to a large degree on the premise that we have a right to get as much as we can for ourselves, many people have unthinkingly tried to integrate this selfish notion with spirituality, and so now think that they may even have a "right" to expect God to give them a return gift because they have given Him a part of their lives.

Carl Jung describes the psychology underpinning these

difficulties with worship in this passage (already quoted in part in Chapter 4):

> When, therefore, I give away something that is "mine," what I am giving is essentially a symbol, a thing of many meanings; but owing to my unconsciousness of its symbolic character, it adheres to my ego, because it is part of my personality. Hence there is, explicitly or implicitly, a personal claim bound up with every gift. There is always an unspoken "give that thou mayest receive." Consequently the gift always carries with it a personal intention, for the mere giving of it is not a sacrifice. It only becomes a sacrifice if I give up the implied intention of receiving something in return. If it is to be a true sacrifice, the gift must be given as if it were being destroyed. Only then is it possible for the egoistic claim to be given up. Were the bread and wine simply given without any consciousness of an egoistic claim, the fact that it was unconscious would be no excuse, but would on the contrary be sure proof of the existence of a *secret* claim. Because of its egoistic nature, the offering would then inevitably have the character of a magical act of propitiation, with the unavowed purpose and tacit expectation of purchasing the good will of the Deity (pp. 256-257).

This passage is rich in meaning for our topic. Jung is saying that, from a psychological point of view, it is not only fruitless to sacrifice the bread and wine to God as a matter of obligation, unconscious of their meaning to us, but that it is *dangerous*. If we are going to give God this gift, he says, we had best be aware of what we are doing, otherwise we will be caught in the trap of giving Him the gift in an attempt to buy His love or forgiveness.

When we act from this motive, no matter how unconscious it might be, our spirituality descends from the heights of Christ's to a kind of magic: we prepare our gifts, we say some words, and, *voila!*, we expect to have God's love.

This attitude is a violation of the psychological integrity of the people who have it, not to speak of the spiritual integrity of the Eucharist itself. It creates in people's minds a false notion of who they are, Who God is, and all that this world and their lives mean. Out of this false notion can come all kinds of religious problems and psychological confusions. Even physical ailments can result from this unconscious attitude, for the mind and the spirit are connected with and affect the body in real ways. The most important thing that Jung says on this topic, however, is that these people *choose* these problems when they choose unconsciousness. It is as if when we choose to celebrate Eucharist we raise the stakes of our lives: we can win more, but we can also lose more.

This passage also explains another difficulty that many people express regarding religion in general: they say they can see no reason for worshiping God other than the fact that He wants us to "feed His ego," as it were. He wants us to feel that His blessing and protection are important and, in our desperation for His approval, He wants us to "buy" them with worship. These people continue that since it is not right for God to ask such a thing, or for people to do such a thing, they refuse to worship Him at all.

From the standpoint of healthy psychology, Jung agrees that this motive for worship would be wrong. However, he says that he does not see the problem in God but in the people who think this way—to be specific, in their choice to be unconscious of their "secret claim" for a return gift, which is revealed in the very fact that they do not know what their gift means to them. Unaware of the meaning of their gift, they are also unaware of how much they are attached to it, and so they are unaware of what they want for it in return. Since this thought process is unconscious, they easily project the entire problem onto God. He becomes the villain Who is looking for gifts to satisfy His ego, and they can be righteous in their own minds by not feeding the ego of such a voracious Deity.

When we examine these ideas from the point of view of consciousness, however, the entire situation is turned upside down. It is not that these people do not need God and therefore do not need to worship Him. They need worship and God as much as anyone else. Specifically, they need Eucharistic worship, for that is exactly the form of worship that will call them to consciousness regarding their egoistic claims on their own lives. The self-sacrificial nature of Eucharist would be able to help them give up these claims, and the result of doing so would be a greater freedom to grow in maturity on both the psychological and spiritual levels. If they allow themselves to stay in their unconscious attitudes, they will be founding their lives on rebellion against God and a resultant egocentrism, all masquerading as healthy independence and maturity. The masquerade is only possible because they are unconscious of their true feelings.

Living this way is like trying to build a house on a foundation of sand (cf. Mt 7:21-27), for in it the only basis for a person's life is that which is human, and human beings are ever-changing. If we want to build our lives on rock and live in harmony with ourselves, others, and our world, it is important to be in unity with Reality, with the Center of the universe.

Another difficulty some people have with Eucharist is similar to the one we have just investigated. These people say that since Eucharist does not "feed" them (usually this means that the celebration does not give enough emphasis to Bible teaching, and maybe also to praise in joyful song and spontaneous prayer), they will need to find another church that does. So they leave their home church to find another that offers them the excitement of mind and spirit they say they need, but usually it is not a "Eucharistic" church—that is, one for whom Eucharist is a central experience.

Some of the feelings these people have are founded in reality. Self-sacrifice, which is the heart of Eucharistic celebration, often does not appear to feed people, especially to feed their minds. And it is also true that scriptural teaching is not the centerpiece in Eucharistic celebrations that it is in non-Eucharistic churches.

But if it is true food for the spirit which these people seek, they could not find a richer banquet than in Eucharist. When praise and receiving God's Word prepare us to sacrifice ourselves to the Father as Christ did, our spirits are truly fed in Eucharistic celebration as they can be in no other way. When we empty ourselves through self-sacrifice so that God can fill us with Himself in Communion, two things may happen. On the one hand, being filled with God can be a spiritual consolation unequaled in religious experience; but, on the other hand, the experience of emptying ourselves may not yield such a consolation—we have examined at length how the process of sacrifice can be painful because it is a process of self-awareness. However, when we sacrifice ourselves sincerely, no matter how we may feel, it is, as Jung says even from a psychological point of view, "the real thing" (p.261).

One may ask of these people, then, whether their real intent is "to be fed" or "to feel good." Surely it never feels good to sacrifice ourselves, but it does feed our spirits with true spiritual food. Sacrificing ourselves to God may seem somber to some, but it also seems to be what we human beings need most to counteract the selfishness that reigns in our lives without it.

The ultimate goal of true religion, then, is furthered by Eucharistic self-sacrifice—that is, to seek God and God alone, so that He becomes our sole inheritance (Ps 16:5). It is only as we sacrifice parts of our lives frequently, even daily, that our lives begin to be God's and not only our own, so that finally we own nothing that is not also God's, so that we are emptied of our selfishness and we remain empty until God comes. As the Scriptures hauntingly ask of us so frequently, what else would we need if we were filled with God?

Furthermore, when the practice of self-sacrifice is eliminated from religion, religion becomes monstrous, for it teaches people how to give to God *in order to* receive. This is a parody of true religion, for there is little dedication to God in it, only selfishness in the name of religion. In certain circles, however, this attitude seems to be popular today. We can find it as we examine the implicit expectations in a variety of theologies that have been called the Prosperity Gospels, or the Health and Wealth Gospels, which are preached today in various churches and on several religious radio and television shows.

These theologies teach in one way or another that if people are dedicated to God and give their lives to Him, they should want for no good thing, and God will hear and answer all their prayers in the very same way in which they are prayed. In some of these teachings, people are even encouraged to remind God over and over again of a promise He has made to us in the Bible until He fulfills it. While there is nothing wrong with persistence in prayer and even Jesus encouraged us to pray this way (Lk 18:1-8), this kind of teaching also implies something else very different—namely, that we deserve to receive anything we want if we stand in righteousness before God.

While they are based on certain Bible texts, these doctrines take the words of Christ out of context and twist their meaning into a pleasing Gospel that satisfies people's baser instincts. They tell people that their lives are meant to be blessed in every way *they* want, and that God has little to say about it as long as their desires are moral—that is, within the parameters of God's law. Thus these doctrines encourage people to relate to God legalistically as well as without humility. Indeed, after adopting these teachings many people find themselves in the psychological position of God, for they get to tell God what to do, while God must obey them, if they have followed the rules that, supposedly, He has set down. Somehow, everything becomes confused, for in true religion it is we who need to obey God if we want to grow in spiritual life.

And, if it were true that the righteous person could ask anything from God and receive it, Jesus Himself would never qualify as a dedicated Christian, for He was poor, harried, without faithful friends, and in the end, when He needed God's help the most, the Father did not answer His prayers to be spared. Since it is Eucharist that forces people to face the reality of selfless sacrifice as Jesus lived it, we can see how teachings like the Prosperity Gospels could only take hold in non-Eucharistic hearts. It is a teaching of receiving. The Eucharist teaches us to give to God without expecting anything in return. While this is not often a pleasant experience, it continues to be the real thing.

The spirituality that underpins Eucharist—sacrificing ourselves to God without expecting a return gift—is the only true food for the spirit, for it yields a blessing in conversion, transformation, renewal, and healing without measure. It is the only enduring path to spiritual life. Those who go elsewhere for it are leaving a banquet that provides it all. When we hear God's call to consciousness and holiness, the Eucharist takes on all the meaning we need, indeed, more than that to which we can often respond. We are richly fed at this table.

Sometimes the most uncomfortable thing we can do is honestly to face our deepest feelings, attitudes, opinions, and difficulties, for doing so means we must admit all that they reveal about ourselves as well as about our strengths, weaknesses, and values. Since the Eucharist is Jesus Himself, Who is the Way, the Truth, and the Life (Jn 14:6), when we face the Eucharist honestly our secret, unconscious, selfish, and wounded selves are revealed, not just so that we can see who we are, but so that Jesus can love us into the person He knows we can become. That is the work and the gift of Eucharist.

Nothing can be more fearsome and awesome than to face truth. But in our hearts we know that only truth will satisfy us, heal us, transform us, renew us, humanize us, and fulfill our heart's desires. That truth could be explained in many books which we might do well to read. But the complicated truth of nature, humanity, and divinity is most completely expressed in one sacred symbol and sign, the Eucharist, the Sacrament of God's love. It is constantly with us for our wonder and worship.

AN OUTLINE FOR EUCHARISTIC CELEBRATION

As an aid to those who plan to use the approach to Eucharistic celebration described in this book, an outline of the approach is presented here. The outline follows the rite of Eucharist as it is celebrated in the Roman Catholic Church, explaining how a participant can pray during each part of the celebration for the self-sacrifice in union with Christ that leads to transformation, renewal, and healing. It presents only the essentials of the approach, eliminating complications for the sake of simplicity, and leaving the nuances for further study and application.

This outline may be helpful in studying this approach in preparation for Eucharist, or as an aid to prayer in actual celebration of Eucharist the first few times this approach is used. It may also be helpful to celebrants who wish to teach this approach to Eucharist to their congregations as a psycho-spiritual guide to the structure of Eucharistic celebration; they will probably find this outline most helpful when it is used in conjunction with Appendix B, "Notes for Celebrants."

Preparations Before Eucharistic Celebrations

A. Become quiet within, and center on the power of Jesus in your life.

B. Decide on your "personal theme" for this Eucharist.
C. Bring to mind all the aspects of this issue that you can think of, both physical and interior.
D. Heighten your awareness of these aspects of the situation as you prepare for the celebration to begin.

I. *The Opening Rite*

A. With your "personal theme" in the forefront of your mind, praise God in song and word. Praise God with this issue, not in spite of it. Remember, it is a part of your life and/or someone else's, and so God loves it, and He created it to be good.
B. During the Penitential Rite, ask God's forgiveness regarding any selfishness or other sinfulness involved with this issue. Trust Him to forgive you and thus open you to more of His love.

   1. Let go of any desire for a return gift in exchange for the gift of your life.
   2. Ask how the *participation mystique* is at work in you, and ask to be freed of it.

II. *The Liturgy of the Word*

A. Continuing to be aware of your "personal theme," listen to God's Word. Allow the Word to permeate, to saturate this issue in your life.
B. Listen for what God wants you to hear through these readings from the Bible: hope, consolation, encouragement, correction, wisdom, guidance, deeper insight into your "personal theme."
C. Allow God's Word to bring you to greater consciousness regarding this issue, so that you are more aware of the meaning this issue has in your life.

III. *The Liturgy of the Eucharist*

A. During the Preparation of the Gifts, bring your "personal theme"—now heightened in consciousness—to the altar with the bread and wine.

    1. Prayerfully and intentionally, unite the physical aspects of this issue with the bread.
    2. Unite the psychological and spiritual aspects with the wine.
    3. Be aware of how much your gift means to you (*participation mystique*), and give it to God precisely because it means so much.

B. During the Eucharistic Prayer, unite with Christ's perfect attitude of self-sacrifice by offering your "personal theme" to the Father with His sacrifice of His life and love. Let His attitude humanize yours.

    1. At the Words of Consecration, believe that what you have prayerfully united with the bread and wine enters into the heart of Jesus.
    2. Continue to give control of this issue to Jesus, so that His love can permeate it and transform it (breaking the *participation mystique*).

C. During the Doxology and especially as everyone proclaims the Great Amen, let your heart praise God for the renewal coming into this area of your life, even if you may not yet be aware of exactly what He is doing to renew it.

IV. *The Communion Rite*

A. During the Our Father, ask that Jesus' perfect attitudes become more your own.

1. Sacrifice your ego as you allow His values preeminence in your life.
2. Open yourself to becoming more firmly attached to the Body of Christ.

B. During the Rite of Peace, ask that Jesus' actions be shown through your own.

1. Choose to reach out to everyone as Jesus would—just because they are there—bonding yourself to the entire Body of Christ.
2. Ask that the way you live may more closely conform to the way He did so that you are prepared to be totally one with Him in Communion.

C. As the celebrant presents the Body and Blood of Jesus for worship, let your response be one of total belief that He can and will renew your life in this particular area through this Communion with Him ("only say the word and I will be healed").

D. As you receive Communion, believe you are receiving the renewal and transformation of this "personal theme" as you receive the bread and wine.

1. Gratefully receive the grace (God's life) for the renewal of the physical aspects of the issue as you receive the bread.
2. Gratefully receive the grace (God's life) for the renewal of the emotional and spiritual aspects as you receive the wine.
3. If you only receive the bread, believe that Jesus is completely present in it, able to bring the renewal you need
4. The *participation mystique* is broken, so what God returns to you can now be filled with Him, since it is not filled with yourself.

5. You also are receiving into your heart everyone else who has participated in the Eucharist, bonding yourself more tightly to the Body of Christ.

E. As you pray after Communion, ask God to reveal to you what He is doing for the renewal of your "personal theme" so that you can cooperate with Him as He does it.

V. *The Dismissal Rite*

A. Thank God for what He has done.
B. Choose to be a more vibrant part of the Body of Christ in the world.
C. Gratefully receive His commission to give Eucharistic love to others.

NOTES FOR CELEBRANTS

Celebrants of the Eucharist are in a unique position to help people find deep meaning and value in the Lord's Supper. Not only by the attitude with which they celebrate the sacrifice and the care they give to it, but also through various comments they can make throughout the celebration, they can help people experience Eucharist more deeply as a Sacrament of renewal and transformation.

Particularly regarding the view of Eucharist presented in this book, celebrants can be extremely helpful to the congregation during the actual ceremony of worship by pointing out the structure of the celebration, and by suggesting ways in which the congregation could use the various parts of the celebration for transformation and renewal, both personal renewal and renewal of other people as well as issues of concern for them.

For example, before the ceremony begins, or just after the opening hymn, the celebrant can ask the congregation to think of a part of their lives they are going to sacrifice to God at this Eucharist, thus establishing their "personal theme" for the celebration. Without any or much explanation, this will make sense to most everyone, and it will help them focus their minds on a way they can come to God with heightened consciousness for self-sacrifice.

Then, during the Penance Rite, the celebrant can suggest

that all present confess to God the selfishness or other sinfulness in their lives regarding this part of their lives they are sacrificing to God. The celebrant can explain that to the degree to which they selfishly hold on to this area of their lives, God cannot fill it. In a few moments of silence and a simple prayer, they can seek forgiveness, and the celebrant can encourage those present to believe that God indeed has forgiven them and that they indeed are freer now to listen to His Word.

Before the congregation listens to God's Word, the celebrant can suggest to them that God will speak to their hearts through His Word, but only if they expect Him to do so. The celebrant can encourage them to be open to God doing this, and suggest they keep uppermost in their minds the part of their lives they are sacrificing to Him as they listen to His Word. Through receiving God's Word into their hearts, they are allowing Him to take over this area of their lives a little more. The celebrant can encourage the congregation to be open to God's guidance, hope, renewal, correction, and insight through receiving His Word.

Just before or while preparing the gifts of bread and wine, the celebrant can suggest to the congregation that they prayerfully and intentionally unite the physical aspects of their gift with the bread and the interior aspects with the wine, choosing with Christ to give themselves to the Father expecting nothing in return. Just before the Eucharistic Prayer, the celebrant can again suggest that as the bread and wine are transformed into the Body and Blood of Christ, so our personal gifts will be transformed and enter into Jesus' heart so that He can bring them to the Father.

Throughout the Communion Rite, the celebrant has many opportunities to help people understand how they can draw closer to Jesus through these prayers. In introducing the Our Father, the celebrant can suggest that the congregation pray these words slowly so that they can more consciously take on the attitudes of Jesus. In inviting the congregation to share the Sign of Peace, the celebrant can remind all the people that with this rite they make a spiritual pledge to be open to each other in the name of Jesus, and to treat each other as He would, both in the celebration and afterward. As the Eucharist is presented for worship before receiving Communion, the celebrant can encourage the congregation in faith that they can be renewed and healed through Jesus in the Eucharist ("only say the word and I will be healed").

After Communion, the celebrant can encourage everyone to pray and ask God what He is doing to transform and renew the situation each has presented to Him in this Eucharist. As much as possible, the celebrant should encourage people in this kind of prayer at this time, dissuading them from making this their time of petition. And in the Dismissal Rite, the celebrant can encourage the congregation to use the grace God has given in this part of their lives which they have sacrificed to Him.

All these things can be done simply with a congregation that has had no prior preparation in this approach to the Eucharist. If some preparation can be given in the form of homilies or religious education classes, much more can be done to bring a congregation to awareness regarding this most beautiful of celebrations. Celebrants will find as they use this approach that people will express a deeper appreciation and love for the Eucharist, they will become more whole on a psychological level and holier on a spiritual level, and they will have more reasons to be faithful to this Sacrament.